#LeadWell

A 31-Day Leadership Development Devotional

Essential Qualities for Those Who Desire to Lead Well

Reginald M. Holiday

Reginald M. Holiday
Title: #LeadWell: A 31-Day Leadership Development Devotional - Essential Qualities for Those Who Desire to Lead Well

ISBN: 978-1737946205

Printed in the United States of America.
December 2021. First Edition.

Contents

Words of Praise for #*LeadWell*

Reginald Holiday is my friend! While known to many as many things, Reggie is my dear and trusted friend. Because he is a beloved son to the Father, he is my brother. He is son, brother, friend, and only then do we take up the issues of ministry and leadership. In that we *are* friends, I know his heart and motives, the way he thinks, and the burdens of his heart for leaders. These are the realities from which Reginald, our brother, has written his excellent devotional. As I read Reginald Holiday's manuscript, I was struck with the clarity of heart and thought concerning the things that truly matter. Those things would include: The Fatherhood of God; The Centrality, Supremacy and Preeminence of the Son, Jesus Christ; The Sonship of All Believers as True Identity; Agape-Love as the Law of the Kingdom; The Life of Devotion to Jesus Christ; The Need for a True Spirit of Wisdom and Revelation; and Practical Application. All of these are well covered in this rich devotional, called LeadWell. This work will prove to be helpful to multitudes of souls. And it will be helpful to all of us as individuals who choose to follow its principles. It's my joy, honor, and privilege to highly recommend Reginald's apostolic devotional. May our Father use this work to transform the lives of the many. – *Christopher P. Johnson*

Apostle Reginald Holiday has provided a 'how to' on the principles of Leadership Development. He has been able to integrate life experience with biblical scriptures. I recommend this 31-day devotional to any leader who wants to increase their knowledge. - *Dr. Matthew Parker, founder of the Global Summit and Institute of Black Family Development*

I have known and walked with apostle Reginald Holiday for several years. He has a genuine spiritual gift of leadership, as presented in Romans 12:8. I have been amazed at the evidence of diligence and discipline that I have personally observed in his life. He is also a zealous student of the Word of God and is imminently prepared and equipped to offer this teaching on leadership, and I highly recommend it. - *James P. Beck Jr, Master Builders Fellowship Fivefold Team*

This devotional on leadership is both inspirational and instructive and will daily equip leaders who want to press into all God wants from them in these critical times. It will encourage you and spiritually empower your leadership. - *Rev. C. Jeffrey Wright, CEO, UMI (Urban Ministries, Inc.)*

The devotions in this book and the reflections they elicit will be an asset to leaders seeking to grow more effective in any context, by desiring to do so applying solid biblical principles. - *Kevin L. James, Ph.D., CPA, Dean, Willie A. Deese College of Business & Economics, North Carolina A&T State University*

This leadership resource is a must-have for those truly seeking to "Lead Well"! I've personally benefited from the leadership principles in this book as a senior executive. I would highly encourage anyone seeking to pursue excellence in leadership to spend the next 30 days on this journey to lead well! - *James M. Cox, II, CEO, Greensboro Housing Authority*

The Spirit of the Lord, through Paul, an apostle, gave a simple mandate for those who lead and that is, 'with zeal' (Romans 12:8). Apostle Holiday has taken this mandate of leadership by the Spirit not only to heart but also to soul, strength, and mind. He is a man of zeal, and his leadership is marked by it. In *#LeadWell* you will dive deeply into the depths of this man as he has learned and followed in the steps of the greatest of all leaders, Jesus of Nazareth. If you have received the 'gift of grace' to lead, I highly recommend this book to you. Each devotional is a pure nugget of gold on leadership. Each day your heart will be touched, your soul nourished, your strength renewed, and your mind challenged as you lead with zeal for the expansion and advancement of His Kingdom. - *Bob Engel, National Director, World Impact/The Urban Ministry Institute (TUMI)*

I strongly endorse *#LeadWell* because Reginald Holiday leads by example. So much is said about leadership in our culture today, but few self-proclaimed leaders are willing to make the investment in the lives of those around us. Reverend Holiday walks the walk. His heart and actions to see his community and region thrive are an example to all of us. These practical lessons on leadership can strengthen us all to become better leaders in every aspect of our lives. - *U.S. Congressman B. Mark Walker*

I am truly excited about this book, ***#Lead Well***. As I sit here in my home study surrounded by leadership books of all kinds, I am inspired by author Reginald Holiday and his effort to encourage and equip "growing" leaders from his vast experience of "leading by example" and his proven track record over the years. All leaders will benefit from taking this 31-day journey to their next level of leading well. - *Rev. Michael T. Westbrook, President of The Global Summit & President/CEO of Greater Life Inc.*

As I looked at apostle Reggie's "Lead Well," I was both excited and inspired. I enjoyed the format: instructional (Scripture), informational (teaching of principles), revelation (prophetic insight), and practical/applicational (discussion questions). While all these areas represent leadership strengths that apostle Holiday himself possesses and desires to impart to others, he also has an excellent gift for framing questions that lead to further discussion and personal insights on the part of the hearers. I have often believed that one of Jesus' main strengths as a teacher was his ability to design questions that led his disciples into both clear self-analysis while also making them aware of the greater purposes of his Father's Kingdom. Reggie has the gift to accomplish both of these goals as well. I will be obtaining this book for my leaders, and I highly recommend others doing the same. - *Pastor Michael Osminski, Lord of the Harvest Christian Fellowship and Co-Leader, Greater Detroit Partnership*

Dedication

I dedicate this book to my forever wife and ministry partner, Linda - you always had confidence in my ability to lead even when I did not. Thank you for your unending love and support. I also dedicate this to our children: Dominque (Sydnee), Alecia (Gary), Justin (Sophie), and Wesley (all leaders in their own right). And to our grandchildren: Maximillian (who beat us all in returning to the Father), Ava, Brielle, Asher, Lula, Ariel, and Nova (I see leadership already emerging in them). I also dedicate this to my dear mother, Barbara, who, as a single mother, prayed for me to be a leader, and God heard her.

I wish to dedicate this book to all those who mentored me, encouraged me, invested in me, created opportunities, and even took a risk on me. Heaven knows who you are!

I also wish to dedicate this book to all those who have allowed me to practice leadership function on them: the fantastic saints and sons of God who comprise Bethany Fellowship Church and various leaders I have been privileged to teach and train over the years, including the Fivefold Team of Pneuma Ministries International.

Finally, I dedicate this book to every leader who may be discouraged or disgruntled. You are a leader, and as you participate in the process of becoming all you are to be as a leader, things will get better, but most of all, so will you.

Acknowledgments

I wish to acknowledge those who saw leadership function in me, taught me, and allowed me to flourish, and those who prophesied the writing of not only this book but several others to come. Special shout out to Christopher Patrick Johnson, Mrs. Pecolia Leak, Dr. Harvey "Chip" Rice, Dr. Julius Koonce, John Lofton, Keith Wilks, Darrell Williams, Robyn Gool, Tommy Quick, William Thompson, Dr. Gabe Rogers, Reginald J. White, and Christopher J. Harris. You were chief among those who have urged me to write, to help leaders and the Lord's Church. Finally, I acknowledge every person who has encouraged me concerning the urgency of putting pen to paper to help as many as I can now and, hopefully, those who may read what I have written long after I am gone to be with the Father.

I am also very grateful for and acknowledge my editor and writing mentor, Charles Strohmer. Thanks for your patience, toughness, and insight.

Finally, special acknowledgment and thanks to Charles Morris for his encouragement to write this and other books and his writing and publishing expertise.

Foreword

One of the signs of living in a fallen and sinful world is the crisis of leadership. We have a crisis of political leadership that fuels ideological extremes that demonize those of the opposite party. We have a crisis of marketplace leadership, which makes more visible the chasm between the haves and the have-nots. We have a racialized crisis of racialized leadership, showing that the more diverse our nation becomes, the more divided it is. We even have a crisis of spiritual leadership where some very influential and public pastors have experienced a "fall from grace," as the saying goes. Though that saying has some theological challenges, it points to the reality that no place of leadership is safe from the temptations, which lead to corruption and dysfunction. Because sin is both housed in the soul as well as in structures, institutions, and systems, leaders are a prioritized target of our spiritual enemy. If Satan is audacious enough to try to tempt Christ, there is no question that he would have an agenda to go after leaders in all sectors of society.

The totality of the leadership crisis cannot be blamed on Satan alone, though. Because human beings have freewill, we are faced every day with the opportunity to make decisions in alignment with the mission of God or that demonstrate our captivity to sin. Leaders can make decisions based on the fruits of the Spirit, which bring about the empowerment, liberation, and transformation of others. We can make decisions based on the flesh, which can oppress, marginalize, and dehumanize others. Our leadership capacities and characteristics are rooted in our identities. We can lead out of an identity of the beloved, made in the image of God, or we can lead out of the identity of the broken, mimicking a dysfunctional and fallen world. Leadership is about the thread of decisions that are made over time. The question then becomes, will we surrender those leadership decisions to God?

God's desire is for all of humanity to flourish and thrive, to be fruitful and in alignment with God's mission in creation. From the very beginning, in the form of a serpent, Satan worked to get those made in the very image of God off track. This is what sin does; it works to keep the beloved children of God from living, loving, and leading in accordance with God's will. To live, to love, and to lead, then, is a type of warfare. We must commit to battle for a fruitful, purposeful, empowering, and transformative life. This is especially true for leaders.

In Scripture, we see God calling men and women into covenant, into action, and into positions of leadership for His purposes. This calling into leadership is part of God's plan for the redemption of a fallen and sinful world. God calls Noah into leadership so that there might be a restorative remnant on the other side of judgment. God calls Abraham into leadership to point to a new faith family ultimately realized in Christ. God calls Moses through a burning bush and Esther through her cousin Mordecai into leadership so that we see God's liberating mission for the socially and spiritually oppressed.

These and many others God called into courageous and influential leadership. They were not perfect people. They were not qualified by earthly standards. But God called them and used them. The road of godly leadership begins with saying yes to God's call, but it is fulfilled by staying connected to and growing in God over time. Godly leadership is best seen through the best picture of leadership God ever provided, His Son, Jesus the Christ. His declarations and demonstrations are the ultimate roadmap to address the leadership crisis. We need a larger army of leaders who have been made new in Christ and are committed to growing in Him. This is exactly why the resource you are currently reading and developed by Reginald M. Holiday is so important.

Reginald M. Holiday is a proven leader and has equipped and empowered many men and women for leadership in this nation and around the world. He is deeply committed to godly leadership and the social and spiritual transformation that comes from it. As a pastor, author, and small business owner, I am greatly influenced by him. This devotional book combines his years of leadership experience, his compelling insights, and his deep rootedness in the Bible. I encourage you to read this multiple times, that it might strengthen and mature you as a leader, whether you are in the private or public sector. Allow the Scripture references, thoughts, and questions to add new tools and sharpen existing ones in your leadership toolbox. Most importantly, allow God to speak to your soul that you might become the leader God created you to be.

Rev. Dr. Efrem Smith,
Co-Lead Pastor, Bayside Church Midtown,
and Co-Owner, Influential LLC

Introduction:
Where Are Our Leaders?

One does not have to strain too intently to see that our world is in dire need of quality and credible leaders. In every field of endeavor there appears to be a collective cry of "Who will lead us?" The necessity for good leaders is both a biblical and historical one. Whether in the church or families, businesses, government, or other organizations, we understand that entities and institutions rise and fall based on their leaders' effectiveness. Whether national, locally, or personally, good leadership is needed in times of crisis and chaos. People need to know where to turn, who to follow. The question of "Who will lead us?" also implies a concern for the quality and character of those who lead.

The incidences of leadership failure for a whole host of reasons are numerous. We have witnessed leadership failure in the Church and at the highest levels of our nation's government, with tremendous repercussions and implications. From sports to entertainment and beyond, the examples and actions of those who have failed to live up to the high standards of leading well are plenteous and glaring.

In the absence of quality leaders, we experience a leadership vacuum where people are inclined to do things independently or with little collaboration. People may work in groups but with little coordinated effort or effectiveness when the way forward is not clearly defined. Also, leaders may exist who are perhaps ineffective and weak and, in turn, not respected by those seeking guidance. When that is the case, people are inclined to do what benefits them while continuing to ask, "Who will lead us?" The implications of this are dramatically affecting many. Just as nature abhors a vacuum, people detest a lack of credible leaders.

It is an undeniable reality that when leadership fails, in any aspect of life, followers are decimated, scattered, and become open prey for whatever may take advantage of them. The Lord Jesus Christ speaks to this in Matthew 9:36. Upon seeing the multitude, He is "moved with compassion for them, because they were weary and scattered, like sheep having no shepherd." Moved with pity and sympathy for these leaderless people, Jesus is touched by their condition. They were bewildered, harassed, distressed, dejected, and helpless. Having no shepherd meant they had no leader. And in the absence of credible, quality leadership, lawlessness abounds.

The need for leaders to lead well is evident for many reasons, and for them to remain credible, they must embody and exemplify certain timeless qualities. #*LeadWell* seeks to highlight those leadership qualities for readers to reflect on and study over a 31-day period. Some readers may discover some completely new ideas along the way. Others may meet some old traveling companions with which to get reacquainted. In either case, it is hoped that the book will inspire you to grow in ways to take on board qualities that are vital to leading well. One of the considerable benefits of this kind of growth is that it will make you better aware of patterns of behavior to avoid, and if you have fallen into any, how to overcome them.

Leadership development is a process and not an event. Being effective as a leader over the long term requires continued growth. It is what a leader learns, does, and passes on each day that will keep unlocking his or her full potential as a leader. In order to remain effective and productive, leaders must continue to grow in quality ways. This 31-day devotional for leadership development is the "sowing of seed" with the expectation of "a harvest" that will result in you leading well.

This book is not a light version of devotional reading. #*LeadWell* intends to make you dig deep and supplement your regular devotional time. One of the ways I hope you will do that is to go beyond the devotional material to the Father in prayer and further study in the Word of God. I also hope that you will go beyond gaining cognitive knowledge, despite all its benefits, to experiential or applied learning that produces quality change and growth. To improve the quality of those who follow Christ after us (1 Corinthians 11:1), we must influence them through our example. So ready yourself to be challenged, provoked, and experience dramatic increases in your leadership capacity and function.

To conclude, my purpose in writing this leadership development devotional is to encourage and inspire "growing" leaders to continue in their leadership journey. We have not arrived. But when we do reach our destination, we will all give an account of how well we have led. So my purpose in writing is also about stewardship. Those of us gifted, entrusted, and called to lead well must do so as stewards. God determines the measure for leading well, or leading others. I hope that at the end of our time together you will be more and more inclined to grow in such a way that God will commend you for having led well when you reach your destination.

What Is Leadership and Who Is a Leader?

I have had the tremendous and humbling privilege of serving and leading my family, those within the Lord's Church and the marketplace for over thirty years. At some point or another I realized even from an early age that I demonstrated leadership function nearly all my life while not always being aware of this. "Leadership function" is a term I use to distinguish what we do from who we are. Leadership function is the term I use to define the spiritual gifting, roles, and responsibilities entrusted to those who lead. It is about the execution of the multifaceted duties and expectations of this work. Leadership function is about how we utilize what we have been given, learned, or developed to equip and guide others in the fulfillment of particular aims. It is about what we do as leaders.

For those in Christ, our most authentic identity is as sons to the Father. I have found that so many who fail to derive their identity from sonship to the Father draw it from what they do instead of who they are in Him. I am convinced that we all have leadership capacity. But not everyone wants the additional burden and responsibility of leading, especially if there are easier opportunities for just being among the led.

As I look back over my life I was consistently pioneering something I would have to lead. I held management positions in my marketplace roles, which allowed me to exercise my leadership gift through training and development by which I could grow and get better at leading. As an elder, or when helping to restore an aging and dying congregation, or as an establisher of a New Testament church, I always saw the critical need to grow and develop as a leader. I needed knowledge, understanding, wisdom, tools, and skills to put all of this to work in various capacities. My initial shepherding assignment stretched me as a leader and forced me to learn how to turn theory into actual practice. It also motivated me to raise other leaders, something I have now had the privilege of doing in various aspects for over twenty-five years. I thank the Father for those outstanding and gracious individuals who allowed me to "practice" on them over the years. I am in part the leader I am (to whatever degree) due to their graciousness and patience. I am forever indebted to them. As the Lord has allowed me to progress, I am now privileged to lead leaders who lead leaders who lead other leaders in the US and abroad. I have worked in conjunction with many leaders to further or establish many initiatives with domestic and international implications. The opportunity to work with some of the brightest young minds on the planet has also excited me. I especially value these fantastic and younger leaders who, for some reason, allow me to hang out with them.

I only share any of this to the praise and glory of God's name! I remember reading John Maxwell's *Five Levels of Leadership*. Those levels are: (1) Position, (2) Permission, (3) Production, (4) People Development and (5) Pinnacle. At that time, I thought, "I may never get beyond levels one or two!" However, I pressed through Maxwell's book and learned the specific skills needed to move from one level to the next. As I applied his recommendations, I realized that I developed more as a leader, and beyond levels one and two. I poured myself even more into personal growth and improvement with a mind to bring others along. I invested countless hours reading, studying, attending conferences and workshops, taking various assessments, and trying it all out in the laboratory of life along the way. All of this has brought me to this place.

Many others, such as the late Bishop Ithiel Clemmons, the late apostle Otis Lockett, Sr., Bishop John McClurkin, Robyn Gool, and Pete Beck, Jr., have been leadership models and mentors me. They taught me so much and helped me to see and manifest the leader in me. Whatever leader I have been and progressively become is because I have been instructed, influenced, and impacted by so many others. The growth I have experienced through mentorship is one reason why I desire to share the vital qualities that have been a proven part of my leadership success. I pray that those who read and apply this devotional material will experience incredible breakthroughs in their leadership and press beyond where they are now to become all they can be as a leader.

What is leadership?

Having the privilege of teaching and developing and equipping leaders in both Christian and marketplace contexts for over twenty-five years, I define leadership as follows. Authentic leadership is godly influencing through Christ-like example. "Godly influence through Christ-like example," then will serve as our working definition in this developmental devotion. God does gift some individuals with spiritual leadership gifting (Romans 12:8c). It is what they become as they develop that gifting which matters most. Those who lead best do so through Christ-like example and by the influence of their consistent model. Leaders such as this evidence character and skill, transform situations, and inspire others to positive, productive change.

Who is a leader?

A leader is a person of influence who leads by his or her quality example. The character, credibility, competence, and contribution of such leaders single them out. These persons grow in their influence with others and become catalysts, encouraging transformation in others' lives.

Recall we stated that we would use the phrase "leadership function" to delineate more accurately what we do from who we are. Far too many who receive leadership responsibility and function have confused function for identity. Who we are does affect what we do. But what we do is not where we draw our worth, value, and significance. Our true worth, value and, significance are derived from our being a child of God. And there is nothing more significant than that. *You are not what you do.* Understanding this is not to say that we are without imperfection. God is daily perfecting us and making us who it is He wants us to be. There are times, even with our best intentions, we may fail, judge wrongly, or even sin. Repentance is required at times as we own the part of us that needs to be removed or transformed. Yet, we must know that our leadership role does not define our identity. Leadership function may be something the Father gifts us to do. But it is never to be misconstrued as or with who we indeed are.

Day 1 - Lead with Vision

"Where there is no revelation, the people cast off restraint; but happy is he who keeps the law." (Proverbs 29:18)

Throughout Scripture, the persons God called and chose to use were those to whom He gave a vision or a burden or, better yet, a prophetic revelation. In other words, God gave "sight" to those He graced to be visionaries so that those who may lack vision (prophetic revelation) will not perish (Proverbs 29:18). I mainly believe this kind of vision or prophetic revelation is more "big picture" in terms of scope. In general, those who are apostolic or prophetic receive an eternal, panoramic vision, view, or perspective for God's work and the good of His people. Be mindful that prophetic revelation in the New Covenant primarily speaks to that which is potential. In other words, it is a revelation of what could potentially take place in and through the life of those who yield themselves entirely to the Lord. This prophetic revelation from God will prove to be the catalyst, the source of direction, and the encouragement to maintain a leader's commitment to the Father and His call on the leader's life. This God-given revelation will cause leaders to stay faithful wherever this vision will take them, even though what they have received from God will try them until He brings it to pass. See Psalm 105:17-19.

Leadership implies the pursuit of a specific goal or aim or direction. In God's economy, how He directs is through a vision or a prophetic revelation. To be effective in leading well and for the long haul, every leader must have a God-given vision or revelation.

The Father gave me this definition of a God-given vision: "a revelation of His agenda, for His work, through His power, backed by His resources, carried out by His people, all for His glory."

In the Kingdom, God's vision, a real prophetic insight, comes by revelation and not through imitation. See Galatians 1:16; 2:2. The late T. Austin Sparks, a teaching prophet, wrote this about spiritual disclosure: "How important it is that every fresh undertaking in work for the Lord should come by revelation to those chosen for it." Leading in the Kingdom, then, requires a revelation of God's agenda. This is not to say that those who have good, humanly conceived ideas are of no value. Ideas of this nature, especially by those who are yet growing in the Lord and perhaps have not had a revelation from Him, can at times be implemented and blessed. There are even occasions where some serve in a "second chair" role alongside someone with a vision from God. In this instance, their task is assisting with vision implementation. God sometimes uses scenarios such as these to develop these types of leaders. Ultimately, those tasked with leading do best when they lead with a revelation of God's agenda.

Receiving God's revelation requires a willingness to seek the Father, trust Him, have patience, and an accurate and growing understanding of the process of God as it pertains to receiving that which He desires. Leaders cannot be full of themselves and hope to accept what He can provide. To receive from Him, they must empty themselves, die daily to self, and desire what He wants and requires above anything else.

Also, His revelation is most often progressive. He will not grace you with the totality of what He desires all at once. Expect to be prepared for a progressive unfolding. Expect God to do "His work" in you and on you as He works through you and reveals more of His plan. And be mindful that this process will continue beyond the initial onset of receiving revelation. Remember that Joseph was tested by the revelation he received until it came to full fruition. Those God calls to lead and endow with His vision also can expect tests as well.

I believe God's interaction with King David in the Tabernacle building is an excellent example of what it means to lead with vision. David had a sincere desire to build a house for the Lord, but the Lord instructed David that he would not construct it. In place of building the Temple, David was entrusted with a revelation from God by the Spirit that would include the details of the Temple which his son Solomon would construct, and a massive campaign to prepare the resources that building it would require. Read 1 Chronicles chapters 17, 22, 28, and 29. See also First Chronicles 28:11-12, which illustrates further what I mean as it pertains to leading with vision. David gives the architectural plans that he receives "by the Spirit" to Solomon.

Vision is His agenda.

David's story is an example of this. He had to seek the Lord to be sure of His plan. See 1 Chronicles 17:15-27. So, too, we must seek Him for clarity relative to His agenda. We dare not presume to move until we have heard clearly from God. Seeking to understand that to undertake what He has ordained requires a journey of inquiry into obtaining the mind of God concerning His plan.

Vision is for His work.

God is the author of it. He is its chief architect. Anything established is meant to further His agenda and not ours as leaders. Vision is based upon and follows His pattern. Vision clarifies what His work is and what it requires. It stipulates the why, how, what, when, where, and who for getting His purpose done. God has His plan, purposes, and intentions that rank higher than those of men or whatever ulterior motivations they may have. We must endeavor to discover how His vision to us fits within and helps to accomplish His overarching agenda for us. That agenda is His priority. It is what He has obligated Himself to advance, support, defend, and achieve. Read 1 Chronicles 17:3-14. So, as a growing leader, a person must take the time to receive an impartation of His agenda or original intent.

God-given vision is brought about through His power and backed by His resources.

God's power and resources are both supernatural activities. We cannot rely primarily or solely upon our know-how or ability. God's vision must be fueled and supplied by the Spirit of God working through us and on our behalf. This aspect of revelation requires our partnership with the Holy Spirit, allowing Him to lead and tutor and guide us in executing what the Father desires.

This necessitates our requisite growth in acquiring and operating from His riches in glory or His heavenly resources. Our Father makes available all the kingdom resources needed to accomplish what He has ordained. He is a fantastic Provider and can cause anyone He desires to resource whatever He ordains.

Vision's vehicle is God's people.

His people carry His vision out. See 1 Chronicles 29:1-9. God the Father is ultimately vision's Source of supply. As it pertains to completing His work, God's people serve as the conduits, resource providers, and instruments for His initiatives. He, in His wisdom, chooses to work through His people (Exodus 35:4-29).

Vision must be applied or executed.

As I often say, "Vision without execution is only an exercise in futility." Those who receive His vision are obligated to obey His revealed will. Read Habakkuk 2:1-4. Those through whom our Father chooses to work must meet His criteria, for they are His choice. He works through people, but they are the right people. Most notable about those that God chooses to use is that they are more inclined to depend on the spiritual over the natural to carry out a vision. In other words, our help and power for vision execution primarily come from the Spirit of the Lord. See Zechariah. 4:6.

God-given vision is for His glory.

Effectuated revelation ultimately makes the God of the Bible clear and visible. In other words, it makes Him look good! Someone defined glory as a visible manifestation of the invisible nature of God. Vision manifested gives an accurate representation of the God who is squarely behind it. In whatever capacity you lead, endeavor to do so with a prophetic revelation from God. *Lead with vision.*

Questions: How do you define vision? How will you now define it based on what you have just read? Write the definition of a vision based on today's reading. How does this affect your thinking and, hopefully, your behavior about what God unveils?

Do you have a God-given vision? If so, write it out where you keep your written thoughts. If not, prayerfully consider engaging in the necessary steps to receive a vision from God and His implementation plan.

Application: What steps will you take to "lead with a vision," knowing what you now know about vision?

Prayer: *Father, I pray that the eyes of my heart be enlightened and that You enable me to see as You see (Ephesians 1:17-19). Remove the scales from my eyes and help me empty myself of personal ambition and desires that conflict with Yours. Grant me a revelation of the vision You have assigned to me. Whatever I am and whatever I pursue, I want it to come out from You, advance Your righteous cause and bring You tremendous glory. Amen.*

Day 2 - Lead Prayerfully

"But we will give ourselves continually to prayer and to the ministry of the word." (Acts 6:4)

"As they ministered to the Lord and fasted, the Holy Spirit said, "Now separate to Me Barnabas and Saul for the work to which I have called them. Then, having fasted and prayed, and laid hands on them, they sent them away." (Acts 13:2-3)

It almost goes without saying that prayer must be the basis, the foundation, for leading well. A spiritual or Christian leader's call belongs to Christ and is first ministry to the Lord. Prayer is about intimacy, relationship, and fellowship. It includes worship, confession, repentance, forgiveness, petition, and intercession. In other words, prayer is relationship-based. I cannot stress this too much. We read Jesus instructing the disciples to pray to the Father in Matthew 6:10. Quality and consistent communication with our Father in the name of the Son is of the utmost importance. In its simplest terms, prayer is two-way, faith-filled communication between God's people and their Lord.

We see in Acts 6:4 that the apostles prioritized prayer. Their commitment to prayer demonstrates that leaders must live a lifestyle of intercession, fasting, and prayer. I am so thankful for the host of individuals who taught me early on what they called the worth and work of prayer. For the godly, Spirit-filled leader, prayer has or is becoming more of a joy and a pleasure. Leaders such as these have also embraced the grace-filled work that goes into this Spirit-led, two-way communication with God.

Leading prayerfully is about seeking the Lord, fellowshipping, and communing with the Holy Spirit. I see people who earnestly pray in this manner as being houses of prayer. Leaders who desire to be houses of prayer for the Lord consistently inquire of the Lord as to His will. Those in the Bible whom the Lord used were persons or leaders who prayed. Consider Moses, Joshua, David, Daniel, and Paul as worthy examples.

Leading from a posture of prayer may require the leader to learn to wait patiently for the Father's response, and then yield to the Father's decision. An example of this is King David, who desired to build a house for the Lord, Nathan the prophet informed David that God would instead erect a house for David. God promised David not a physical dwelling but that He would raise after David a descendant, "who will be of your sons; and I will establish his kingdom. He shall build Me a house, and I will establish his throne forever" (1 Chronicles 17:11-12). God was speaking of Christ. Having heard from the Lord, David then sat before the Lord, after the word from Nathan, in prayer, praise, and thanksgiving. Praying leaders thank the Lord after receiving a word from Him.

Personally, praying and waiting are challenging. Most leaders are doers and want to get things accomplished. There have been times that my impatience cost me when instead of praying and waiting I acted before hearing from the Lord. On a few occasions, instead of praying about involving someone in a particular ministry and waiting to see what the Lord would reveal, I entrusted the role to someone, and it did not turn out well. Lessons like this are costly. Learning from such experiences only helps us to lead better.

Jesus is always our Example in all things (1 Peter 2:21; 1 John 2:6). We can learn volumes from His prayer life. Jesus was prone to get alone with His Father. He would pray many times early in the morning. See Matthew 14:23; Mark 1:35; 6:46; Luke 5:16.

This next section would be an excellent place for you to grab your Bible and reflect on it as you read each reference concerning Jesus Christ as our Example in prayer:

- Luke 3:21 - He prayed at His baptism and the initiation of His earthly ministry.
- Luke 5:16 - He would steal away from the crowds, especially after intense ministry.
- Luke 6:12 - He sought the Father all night concerning who His twelve apostles should be.
- Luke 9:18 - Prayer was a lifestyle with Jesus. He often prayed between His ministry or teaching opportunities.
- Luke 9:28-29 - His disciples would often join Him in prayer. Leaders, too, should join in prayer with others, regularly modeling that and teaching it to other leaders and God's people.
- Luke 11:1 - His prayer life was a catalyst for others who desired to learn to pray consistently.
- Luke 18:1 - A life of total dependency on God is the key to not losing heart.

- Luke 22:32 – Jesus prayed with prophetic insight for His closest followers.
- Luke 22:41-44 – Prayer helped sustain Jesus in the most challenging times of His life as a leader.
- Luke 22:40, 45-46 – He commanded the apostles to wake up and pray to overcome temptation, teaching them that prayer would keep them from falling.
- Luke 23:34, 46 – Jesus prayed for His offenders and committed Himself to the Father through prayer in His most difficult time.

Paul, an apostle, consistently prayed for those who made up the Church.

- Romans 1:9 – Paul states that God is his witness as it pertains to his praying without ceasing for the Romans.
- Ephesians 1:15-16 – Paul's hearing of the Ephesians' faith urges him to continuously pray for them, giving thanks for them while mentioning them in his prayers.
- Ephesians 3:14 – Paul expresses his motivation to bow his "knees to the Father of our Lord Jesus Christ" on behalf of the saints. Reading the remainder of that Ephesians chapter helps us see what his prayer for them entailed.
- Colossians 1:9 – The faith, hope, and fruitfulness of the Colossians are part of Paul's enthusiasm to pray ceaselessly for them. He desired that they "be filled

with the knowledge of His will in all wisdom and spiritual understanding" and more (Colossians 1:10-12).

- 1 Thessalonians 3:10 - Paul and his team desired to see the Thessalonians so much that they prayed "*exceedingly*" (with intense earnestness) night and day for it to be so. They wanted to visit them to perfect what was lacking in their faith.
- 2 Timothy 1:3 - Gratefulness and Spirit-filled worship accompanied Paul's prayer for his spiritual son Timothy, whom he remembered night and day in his prayers.

Paul did more than claim to pray both day and night for others. He actually did it. He always prayed for the churches and those he was fathering.

Leaders must pray for direction, grace, strength, and resources. The faithful leaders of the Bible were all individuals who engaged in much prayer. Take a moment and read and meditate on 2 Chronicles 26:5. Leaders remain successful as they keep prayer at the forefront of their lives, and our example in prayer will positively influence those we lead and those with whom we co-labor.

Every leader should be convinced that leadership success is fleeting if it does not entail consistent prayer. I was born again at a church that had a significant call to pray. We were all trained and expected to know the work and worth of prayer. However, praying as a church member was quite different from praying as a leader in that church. This difference became more substantial when I was called upon to lead a congregation, disciple them in a life of prayer, and teach them to lead with prayer. I soon learned that every time I experienced failure, it was when I had failed to pray or pray enough. Instead, I acted or led without seeking the Lord, and it cost me. There were times when I was facing a critical decision about what opportunities to pursue or actions to take. There were other times when I was facing an important decision about whether to appoint a leader. Things rarely go well when we do not pray or pray enough. When I did not pray or pray enough, outcomes were less than desirable, and I was tested by my failure to pray or pray enough and compelled to pray to figure out what went wrong and what to do next.

One such time was when we were hosting a significant community event. Before this particular occasion, we had experienced considerable success with this event, reaching hundreds in outreach and ministry for the Lord. But one year, I assigned someone to lead without really praying it through, and we had a colossal failure. Nothing worked as it had before. The following year, we bathed the event in prayer, and those who would lead it and serve in it, and we regained our former success, even surpassing it. Lesson learned. When we lead without sufficient praying, we set ourselves up for failure, as we try to carry things out independently.

I would suggest that wherever prayer is commanded of or instructed for Christ's disciples, this should be a foundational and super imperative to those called to lead. Leaders desirous of leading well must be committed to leading with prayer.

Questions: How do you personally define "a lifestyle of prayer?" Consider the prayer life of Jesus and Paul. What other praying biblical leaders come to your mind? How do you need to adjust your present prayer life so that it mirrors theirs?

Why is prayer so crucial to you as one who desires to lead well? How should you pray as it pertains to your desire to be one who meets the Master's approval?

Application: Schedule or maintain a regular daily time for prayer. Consider praying morning and evening, like Paul. Also, consider establishing seasons of concentrated prayer where you seek to pray over several hours. Establish an accountability partner who will regularly check with you to ensure you keep your commitment to prayer. Identify others with whom you can pray and even disciple in prayer. And, if you do not already, consider keeping a prayer journal, recording your prayers, prayer requests, and the Lord's responses.

Prayer: *Father, thank You for the privilege and responsibility of prayer. I humbly ask You to make my heart a house of prayer and give me a heartfelt love for all types of prayer. Help me to see prayer as joy and through Your eyes. Teach me to pray for those You have entrusted me to lead as well as to model prayer before them. Thank You for helping me to live a lifestyle of prayer. Amen.*

Day 3 - Lead with Integrity

"So he shepherded them according to the integrity of his heart . . ." (Psalm 78:72a)

When we look for leaders we look for those we can trust. We want leaders whose words and deeds agree. Leading with integrity requires this quality.

A good definition of "integrity" is: consistency in one's words and actions or trustworthiness. And for the godly leader, this kind of consistency must include moral soundness, purity, uprightness, and honesty.

God-ordained leadership leads with integrity. What this boils down to is good, old-fashioned honesty and trust! God's people, rightfully so, should expect and receive honesty from their leaders. Henry and Richard Blackaby write in the book *Spiritual Leadership*: "Followers don't expect their leaders to be perfect, but they do expect them to be honest."

Integrity is the foundation of the confidence that followers place in leaders. Integrity is integral to credibility.

Respected leadership experts and authors of *The Leadership Challenge*, Kouzes and Posner, have used another term for integrity in a leader: credibility. Kouzes and Posner surveyed several thousand individuals and conducted several case studies from around the world. *The Leadership Challenge* reveals that credibility, which goes hand in hand with integrity, was the most frequently cited trait of a good leader. Integrity plus honesty equals credibility. "Credibility is the foundation of leadership. Period," Kouzes and Posner declare. Kouzes and Posner note that the "ultimate test of leaders' credibility is whether they do what they say." Integrity boils down to consistency, and as leaders, this means our doing what we say. Integrity answers the question: do we keep our word, our commitments, and are we like that all the time, even when no one is around?

The whole-life integrity the Bible talks about does not come overnight. It takes time to develop, and, importantly, it begins by keeping your word even with the small things. For example, you're on the phone with someone, or talking with someone at church, and you say, "Let's get together for lunch sometime." Do you follow up on that? Or do you let it slide? With the one, you are keeping your word. With the other you are not. The same holds true for any number of passing comments we make. Be alert to these and what they imply.

The Bible also uses the word "blameless" for those who walk in integrity. See 1 Timothy 3:2. The expectation of those who lead is to be "blameless."

WORD INSIGHT

Blameless (Strong's 677) (aproskopos from a = not + proskopto = strike at, to trip, dash against as foot against a stone) literally means without offense, without stumbling, not stumbling, or not tripping. Not causing others to

> stumble or fail. Not giving offense (thus inoffensive). Aproskopos describes "relational integrity," meaning that Christians are to live lives of true integrity that do not cause others to stumble. It is blameless in the sense of not offending or not causing someone else to stumble. It describes one who does not lead others into sin. Such a one is inoffensive and clear (in their conscience). (*Precept Commentary*)

I believe Daniel is another excellent example of integrity. "Then this Daniel began distinguishing himself among the commissioners and satraps because he possessed an extraordinary spirit, and the king planned to appoint him over the entire kingdom" (Daniel 6:3). Daniel was recognized above all others due to his integrity as a leader. People think about us by reputation. But God knows us by character and integrity. Daniel possessed both. He understood that who a man is in and before God is who that man truly is. See Proverbs 15:3.

What else does the Bible say?

- Proverbs 11:3 – Integrity directs the upright.
- Proverbs 12:22 – The Lord delights in the trustworthy but detests liars.

- Proverbs 21:3 – Walking in integrity is more pleasing to God than any sacrifice.
- Proverbs 28:6 – Integrity without wealth is better than riches without integrity.
- 2 Corinthians 8:21 – Paul instructs us to put forth increasingly faithful effort in doing what is right, not for the sake of men but for the Lord.
- Hebrews 13:18 – Those who would walk in integrity desire to live in a God-honoring way, and they ask others to pray for them that they live this way.
- 1 Peter 3:16 – Endeavor to keep a clear conscience, as this is the antidote to those who would slander us.

Questions: What biblical leaders can you think of who exemplified integrity? How would you rate your own truthfulness? Is there an area, or areas where you struggle with this the most? What steps can you take to improve your personal integrity?

Application: Ask the Father what He thinks of your integrity and ask for the grace to make improvements and changes necessary to be pleasing to Him. Study what the Word of God says about integrity and seek to apply it to your life. You may want to engage an accountability partner to help you here. Pray that God makes you a person of godly integrity.

Prayer: *Father, integrity is a vital part of who You are. You always keep Your word. As a partaker of Your divine nature, I pray that I exhibit integrity consistent with who You are in me. Forgive me for lapses in my personal and leadership integrity. I* *pray that I consistently demonstrate the integrity of my heart in all my dealings. And help me to be among those who lead with integrity in every aspect of life. Amen.*

Day 4 - Lead with Skill

". . . And guided them by the skillfulness of his hands." (Psalm 78:72b)

"Skillfulness" is about intelligence or understanding, as well as discretion, reason, and wisdom. Found first in Genesis 25:27, the word "skillful" speaks of Esau's exceptional skill as a hunter. Esau was genuinely knowledgeable in hunting. This knowledge came through experience or perception over time. Skills are acquired and developed in the life of every leader. As with Esau, we grow as skilled leaders through experience. But experience alone is not the best teacher. Applied experience is the best teacher. We grow as leaders from our experience or from the experience of others, and then we utilize that as warranted as we press ahead.

We also develop our skillset through perception. "Perception" can be defined as "the quality of being aware of things through the physical senses, especially sight," or "the ability to notice and understand things that are not obvious to other people" (*Cambridge English Dictionary*). Based on these two aspects of what perception means, skillful leaders will be attentive and observant. By perceiving, they learn in ways that help them execute their leadership function. As you can see, being a capable leader is not a simple task. It requires time, experience, and intentionality.

As a "pattern leader," David led God's people with "the skillfulness of his hands." But what does this mean?

David developed his skill as a leader over time. He gained many valuable experiences and increased perception along the way. Psalm 78:72 says that David "guided them." "Guide" means to "lead or to lead forth." The Psalm says that in leading the Lord's people, King David led them forth with intelligence, understanding, discretion, reason, and wisdom. Where did he acquire this? Most definitely from the Lord as well as from his own experiences and perceptions.

There are a plethora of skills that leaders must have and need to develop or improve to lead well. Every leader's essential skills include communication, empathy, creativity, problem-solving, decision making, delegation, active listening, motivation, conflict resolution, time management, teamwork, emotional intelligence, critical thinking, and interpersonal communication. Even taking all these together, we still have an incomplete list of skills that leaders who lead well need in their toolkit.

Another vital aspect of this is to take note of how God graces us with skill. Take time to look at biblical examples of this. For instance, Exodus 35:35, which explains that God fills His workers with skill so that they may do the work He ordains. Daniel 1:17 and 9:22 also show us that God is the Giver of the skills necessary to accomplish His work.

The instruction and equipping of others is a final aspect of developing necessary skills for leading well. I have had the privilege of "sitting at the feet" of many individuals who helped me cultivate much-needed skills as a leader. One of these was the late Ithiel Conrad Clemmons, my first real pastor, and mentor who taught me the importance of knowing how to lead with a solid team. His example, instruction, and encouragement were never to do ministry alone but to select others and get the work done together. Leading this way required developing several skills, including knowing how to identify faithful folk, direction setting, delegation, communication, and more. I believe we will never become the leaders we could be or acquire the skills we need to lead well without the input of others.

My encouragement is to assess your skillset periodically, and if you lack sufficient skills in any of these (just named) areas, find the ways and means to develop them. Pray and ask the Father His opinion, check with others, and evaluate yourself. Leading well requires us to acquire the skills necessary to function consistently and effectively.

Questions: What leadership skills do you already possess? What skills do you lack or need to improve? Why is it vital that you have a plan for continuous improvement as a leader?

Application: How will you implement an annual plan for "skill development or improvement?" I encourage you not to try to develop multiple skills at once. But choose perhaps four each year, and then develop or improve in one of them every quarter. Chart a course for what this requires and have at it. Hold yourself accountable or have an accountability partner and reward yourself for success.

Prayer: *Heavenly Father, I recognize that skill comes from You and from experiences and perceptions. I humbly ask that You equip me with every skill necessary to carry out Your will. I desire to be a faithful steward of what You have already provided.*

Please help me to improve in terms of skillfulness continuously. May the skills You develop in me be for Your glory and the good of Your people. Amen.

Day 5 - Lead with Patience

"And a servant of the Lord must not quarrel but be gentle to all, able to teach, patient." (2 Timothy 2:24)

Patience plays a significant role in the lives of those who desire to lead well. Patience is a critical requirement in multiple aspects of leadership function, which requires growth for the process of developing a leader is not an overnight occurrence. The assignment of leadership takes time. The advancement of vision and of God's people is not an instantaneous matter. Due to their impatience leaders might abort the plan of God for their lives. Leaders must be people of patience.

Writing to his spiritual son and fellow apostle Timothy, Paul urged him to demonstrate patience in dealing with those who are argumentative and perhaps in need of repentance. In this apostolic epistle, Paul deals with leaders who are in error. He states that patience is crucial if leaders want to see those who have been taken captive by the devil come to their senses and be free. See 2 Timothy 2:23-26.

In recent times, more Christians have gotten so caught up in dubious beliefs about politics and nationalism that it can be tough to discuss this with them. These beliefs have created a vast divide among believers, partly because they have not provided "godly edification which is in faith" or fulfilled "the purpose of the commandment (which) is love from a pure heart, from a good conscience, and from sincere faith" (1 Timothy 1:4b-5). There is a need for godly patience in these contexts.

In 2 Timothy 2:24, "patience" better translates into "patient when wronged." Those who lead as servants of the Lord exhibit this patience when they do not see eye to eye with others.

WORD INSIGHT

Patient when wronged (420) (anexikakos from anécho = bear, put up with, holding back + kakós = bad, evil) is literally "holding back under bad or evil." It is tolerating difficulties without becoming out of control or enduring problems without becoming angry or upset. A suitable synonym is "longsuffering." Anexíkakos describes the person who puts up with, patiently forbears, or tolerates evil without resentment and is marked by their forbearance. Patiently enduring what is naturally challenging to bear in terms of others' attitudes and conduct is what is pictured by this term. The Lord's servant must not be contentious but kindly, apt to teach, and "forbearing" even with opponents.

In secular Greek, anexíkakos was used in medicine to describe enduring pain or evil. (*Precept Commentary*)

You can see that the patience we speak of here is supernatural. The fact of the matter is this kind of patience is most accurately a fruit of the Spirit. It is the Holy Spirit that manifests this fruit of patience in and through us.

WORD INSIGHT

"Patience" is one aspect of the fruit of the Holy Spirit (see Galatians 5:22), and it is the Spirit Who provides the inner power we need for bearing this aspect of His fruit. The Spirit-controlled bondservant (see Galatians 5:16; 18; 25; Ephesians 5:18) does not let himself or herself be controlled by injustices done against them, does not harbor these things waiting for an opportunity to take revenge, and is quick to forgive and forget and go on (*Precept Commentary*).

King Saul is an example of an impatient leader who aborted the leadership process. See 1 Samuel 13:1-15. Samuel had instructed Saul to wait for his arrival. But Saul became impatient. He overstepped his bounds as a king and acted in

Samuel's role as priest. Read what the Scripture says resulted from his impatience and disobedience, "And Samuel said to Saul, 'You have done foolishly. You have not kept the commandment of the Lord your God, which He commanded you. For now, the Lord would have established your Kingdom over Israel forever. 'But now your Kingdom shall not continue. The Lord has sought for Himself a man after His own heart, and the Lord has commanded him to be commander over His people, because you have not kept what the Lord commanded you.'" Saul's impatience revealed a significant character flaw, which led to the Lord's rejection of him as king.

Leaders who desire to lead well understand the importance of growing in the discipline of waiting on God for His will to manifest. Such leaders do not want to get ahead of God. They must therefore remain patient and trust the Lord to do those things only He can do. Their task is to trust Him and hold on to His promise, knowing that what He has promised He will bring to pass at His appointed time.

"Patience" in Greek is also endurance. I call it supernatural "hang-in-there power" because it doesn't mean to remain under something with resignation but with vibrant hope.

Look at what these scriptures reveal about that.

- Luke 21:19 – "In your patience possess you your souls."

- Hebrews 6:12 – "Do not become sluggish, but imitate those who through faith and patience inherit the promises."
- Hebrews 10:36 – "For you have need of endurance, so that after you have done the will of God, you may receive the promise."
- James 1:4 – "But let patience have its perfect work, that you may be perfect and complete, lacking nothing."

Clearly, patience is vital to so many aspects of our success in life and leadership. In *Spiritual Leadership*, J. Oswald Sanders writes: "Spiritual leaders need a healthy endowment of patience." It is powerfully essential for those who lead to grow in patience, which will help them avoid the sometimes devastating penalties for impatience. If you truly desire to lead well, lead with patience.

Questions: How patient are you? Are you producing patience as a fruit of the Spirit? What has impatience cost you? What is your plan for situations where you have been impatient?

Application: Leading with patience requires being mindful of where people are within the circumstances that arise, or we may lose our patience. Be very aware of yourself, especially where you lost your patience in the past. Depend on the Holy Spirit to bear this fruit in you, particularly when it is needed. Oswald Sanders also writes, "A leader shows patience by not running too far ahead of his fellow followers and thus discouraging them. While keeping ahead, he stays near enough for them to keep him in sight and hear his call forward." Please take this wise counsel.

Prayer: *Father, thank You for this fruit of Spirit, patience. I understand that You usually teach us patience and manifest patience in us through circumstances where it is required. Please help me to be patient where it is necessary. Especially, allow me to demonstrate patience where I am being wronged. Keep me from suffering the penalty of impatience. In Jesus' name. Amen.*

Day 6 – Lead with Dependence on the Holy Spirit

"Therefore take heed to yourselves and to all the flock, among which the Holy Spirit has made you overseers, to shepherd the church of God which He purchased with His own blood." (Acts 20:28)

Leaders in the New Testament, mostly as depicted in the book of Acts, exemplify what it means to lead with dependence on the Holy Spirit. They knew what it was to be born of the Spirit. They understood the significance of being baptized with the Spirit (Acts 1:8; 2:4). And these leaders knew what it meant to teach the Lord's people to be increasingly dependent on the Spirit of God. Peter, an apostle, was the first to disclose what happened among the disciples on the Day of Pentecost. See Acts 2:14-21. After people repented and were baptized, Peter declared that they would receive the gift of the Holy Spirit (Acts 2:38). From then on, those called and privileged to lead the Church would demonstrate a dependence on the Holy Spirit.

In Acts 20:28, Paul, an apostle, admonished the Ephesian elders that the Holy Spirit had made them overseers. Being Holy Spirit-appointed overseers is consistent for us as well. When it is of God, we understand that our function is made possible by the Holy Spirit. Therefore, it behooves us to be utterly dependent upon Him. My encouragement to you is not just to recognize this but to continue to grow in this.

It was the Holy Spirit that sustained Peter's boldness (Acts 4:8, 31). Even those who were to provide oversight to the food distribution effort were required to be full of the Holy Spirit, controlled by God's Spirit (Acts 6:3, 5). Luke recorded it this way, "Therefore, brethren, seek out from among you seven men of good reputation, full of the Holy Spirit and wisdom, whom we may appoint over this business" (Acts 6:3).

Dependence on the Spirit is, of course, also vital for preaching (Acts 2:14-39; 6:8, 10; 7:1-60). Peter proclaimed that even Christ was anointed with the Spirit: "God anointed Jesus of Nazareth with the Holy Spirit and with power, who went about doing good and healing all who were oppressed by the devil, for God was with Him" (Acts 10:38). If the Lord Jesus Christ was dependent upon the Holy Spirit, how could we also not be and yet hope to lead well?

While prophets and teachers in the church at Antioch fasted and worshipped, the Holy Spirit directed what would occur next by identifying those whom the Lord would send forth in His work. Notice no one had a personal agenda. They were open to the leading of the Spirit, which not only demonstrates that they knew the voice of the Spirit but that they were submitted to the Spirit's guidance (Acts 13:1-3). The early Church's leaders resolved issues according to the wisdom of the Spirit (Acts 15:1-29). They sought approval from the Spirit that which was pleasing to Him. See Acts 15:28.

Even though we may know that we are utterly dependent on the Holy Spirit, sometimes we just get distracted with the busyness of leading. Many years ago, a pastor I know had a leading from the Lord to launch a major "one in the Spirit" rally to bring together churches in his city. Plans for that event were going pretty well for a few weeks, until they began to hit all sorts of unexpected walls and it seemed he hadn't heard from the Lord after all. The breakthrough came when he admitted to himself and then to other leaders, "I've been so busy planning this event and talking to everyone about it that I forgot to talk to the Lord about it!" He then stopped the planning went to prayer for a season. Afterward, the event came together remarkably.

In writing to the Galatians, Paul encouraged them to "walk in the Spirit, and you shall not fulfill the lust of the flesh." He goes on to instruct them, "For the flesh lusts against the Spirit, and the Spirit against the flesh; and these are contrary to one another, so that you do not do the things that you wish." Lastly, Paul writes, "If we live in the Spirit, let us also walk in the Spirit." See Galatians 5:16-17, 25. Dependence on the Spirit means walking in the Spirit.

WORD INSIGHT

Walk (Strong's 4043) (peripateo from peri = about, around + pateo = walk, tread) means literally to walk around, to go here and there in walking, to tread all around. The 39 uses in the Gospels always refer to literal, physical walking. Seven of the eight uses in Acts are also in the literal sense (except Acts 21:21). In contrast, Paul uses peripateo only in the metaphorical sense (thirty-two times), meaning to conduct one's life, to order one's behavior, to behave, to make one's way, to make due use of opportunities, to live or pass one's life (with a connotation of spending some time in a place) (*Precept Commentary*).

George G. Findlay writes that "The walk governed by the Spirit is a spiritual walk . . . The Spirit is not the path in which one walks; rather He supplies the motive principle, the directing influence of the new life. Galatians 5:16 is interpreted by Gal 5:18 and Gal 5:25. To walk in the Spirit is to be 'led by the Spirit'; it is so to 'live in the Spirit' that one habitually "moves" (marches: Galatians 5:25) under His direction" (*Precept Commentary*). Those who lead in this manner are bound to lead well.

What is most true about us is our sonship to the Father. And our sonship is confirmed as the Spirit leads us. We see this in Romans 8:14, "For as many as are led by the Spirit of God, these are sons of God." Considering all of this, we must determine to become more and more dependent on the Holy Spirit. As leaders, we need all that He supplies, including His guidance, knowledge, understanding, wisdom, and power.

Questions: How dependent on the Holy Spirit are you? How do you know when your leadership is a work of the flesh? How can you determine if what you are attempting is in cooperation with the Holy Spirit?

Application: Purpose to seek the Lord daily for a fresh filling of His Holy Spirit. Become more and more reliant on the Holy Spirit. Repent of works done in the flesh and not in partnership with the Spirit of God. How else can you specifically implement or increase your dependence on the Holy Spirit?

Prayer: *Heavenly Father, we know that those who are of the Spirit are to live by the Spirit. So I pray that You will forgive me for not leading as one who has been dependent upon Your Spirit. I repent of functioning in my flesh instead of from the overflow of Your Spirit in and through me. I pray that daily You will freshly fill me with Your Holy Spirit. I thank You that You have made the Spirit available to me and that His abundant supply is there for my success. I ask You to make me a leader who is utterly dependent upon Your Spirit and who has a preoccupation with Him. In Jesus' name. Amen.*

Day 7 - Lead with Diligence

". . . he who leads, with diligence . . ." (Romans 12:8c)

To the saints in Rome with leadership gifts, Paul encouraged them to lead with diligence (Romans 12:8c). What does this mean? What does this require of leaders who desire to lead well?

Kenneth Wuest identifies a leader in Romans 12:8 as "the one who is placed in a position of authority, with intense eagerness and effort." Wuest's translation clarifies two things. One, who leaders are. Two, how we are to lead or what our leadership function entails.

WORD INSIGHT
Leads (Strong's 4291) (proistemi from pro = before, over + hístemi = place, stand) means to put over or before and describes one who is "standing before or over." The figurative sense means to exercise a position of leadership (Romans 12:8, 1Timothy 3:4-5). To place in a position of authority or superintendence. To lead, to preside over to conduct, to direct, to govern, to superintend, or to take over

the direction of the people. According to the one commentary, proistemi also conveys the ideas of being a protector or guardian, giving aid, assisting, caring for, or being active in helping. It brings both clarity and insight to those gifted and set in place when explained in this manner. Leaders ultimately tasked with a great responsibility of stewardship need this understanding to carry this out. The phrase "with diligence" further defines this stewardship of leadership. (*Precept Commentary*)

WORD INSIGHT

Diligence (Strong's 4710) (spoude from speudo = hasten, make haste) refers to eagerness, earnestness, willingness, or zeal. It denotes quick movement or haste accompanying the eagerness, etc., in the interest of a person or cause. Thus, spoude can refer to swiftness of movement or action and means haste or speed (like our expression "in a hurry"). It can refer to an earnest commitment in discharge of an obligation or experience of a relationship. "Spoude primarily speaks of an attitude which is associated with or leads to an action. It conveys the idea of doing something hurriedly (Mark 6:25, Luke 1:39) (but not ineptly) with earnest effort & intense motivation. Clearly, the gift of leadership precludes procrastination & idleness. If you are a lazy leader, the pressure and disappointments of leadership may have caused you to "crawl off the altar." You need to go back to (Romans 12:1) and remember that you are not your own but that you have been bought with a price to glorify God in your body by exhibiting diligent leadership and that one day you will give an accounting for your stewardship (or here) of His gift (Matthew 25:21, 23, Romans 14:12, 2 Corinthians 5:10). (*Precept Commentary*)

What is actually being defined here is an attitude that produces action. It communicates a sense of urgency and with sincere effort and passionate motivation. Clearly, the gift of leadership precludes procrastination and idleness. We see a picture of this in Haggai 1:14, where the leaders and the people are stirred in their spirits by the Lord and resume work on the house of the Lord.

Read the instruction of Ecclesiastes 9:10, "Whatever your hand finds to do, do it with your might; for there is no work or device or knowledge or wisdom in the grave where you are going." Paul gives a similar exhortation in Colossians 3:23-25, "And whatever you do, do it heartily, as to the Lord and not to men, knowing that from the Lord you will receive the reward of the inheritance; for you serve the Lord Christ. But he who does wrong will be repaid for what he has done, and there is no partiality." As you can see, the Old and New Testaments encourage us to be diligent and to recognize the eternal implications of how we do what we do. Diligence is required for those who lead and desire to please the Lord.

Leadership can be complicated and full of challenges. And when it is stretched out over the long term, it can be easy to begin to lose some of the initial zeal and energy. The Scripture encourages us to remain diligent by the Holy Spirit's help, so that we can lead well and finish strong.

Questions: How did you handle times of discouragement and disappointment that made you feel like only going through the motions as a leader? As you consider today's devotion, what is key to maintaining diligence and leading with diligence? How does the definition given for "diligence" help you in your effort to keep it?

Application: With the information you have received, how will you apply it? If diligence is a requirement, what is your "game plan" for remaining diligent in order to overcome feelings of merely going through the motions? When do you find that you are less likely to be assiduous, and how will you manage those occasions?

Prayer: *Father, Your Word has once again challenged me to not only be aware of what You require but to obey You and become and do what will please You. I ask for Your help and grace to remain diligent and to be that way until I stand before You and hear You say, "Well done!" Help me overcome any tendencies of being lazy or letting the leadership load overwhelm me until I do not give leadership my best. I want to lead with diligence every day. So I ask for Your help. Amen.*

Day 8 – Lead Faithfully

"Moreover it is required in stewards that one be found faithful." (1 Corinthians 4:2)

Faithfulness is God's expectation for all those He has entrusted with leadership responsibilities. The aspect of faithfulness that I would like us to focus on in today's devotional is stewardship, for it is required of God's stewards that they all be found faithful. For instance, Paul, an apostle, writing to the Corinthians, clarifies how the Corinthians were to consider apostles: "Let a man so consider us, as servants of Christ and stewards of the mysteries of God" (1 Corinthians 4:1). What Paul writes about apostles should serve as a general standard for all who lead.

A steward is the manager or administrator of the affairs of another. What a steward administrates, he or she must, at some point, give an account. For that matter, all of life is stewardship, and we must steward it faithfully, as one day we will provide an account for it all. Further, since everything belongs to God, we all exercise stewardship in many ways and areas.

WORD INSIGHT
Faithful (Strong's 4103) - trusty, faithful; of persons who show themselves faithful in the transaction of business,

the execution of commands, or the discharge of official duties. (*Thayer's Greek Lexicon*).

But for those called to leadership there are particular concerns. Paul writes that stewards are to be found faithful (1 Corinthians 4:2). Faithfulness is descriptive of how our stewardship is to be carried out and will ultimately be measured. The key is understanding this is that the standard for our fidelity is not ours or anyone else's to determine except God, to whom we must give an account. We see this emphasis in Matthew 25:21, where we read the parable of how one steward has presented himself faithful in managing that which belonged to another. "His lord said to him, 'Well done, good and faithful servant; you were faithful over a few things, I will make you ruler over many things. Enter into the joy of your lord."

Notice this servant has been faithful over a few things. Contrary to popular belief, we will not become more faithful when we come into more if we are not faithful in little things. Not too long after being born again, I was asked to teach a men's small group Bible study. Although this was an infrequent opportunity, I did my best to faithfully prepare for it as though I was the regular facilitator. Little did I know, I was being tested. The result of the testing was that I was assigned to teach a young adult small group every week. I was told that because I had been faithful on those rare occasions, along with my attendance in that class, I was now being entrusted with this new opportunity. Faithfulness in the little things pays off.

We are either growing or diminishing in our faithfulness with each assignment. I am convinced that the Lord promotes the faithful, those who have stewarded well whatever He has graciously assigned to them. This verse makes this case. The reward of this servant in Matthew 25:21 is increased responsibility because of his faithfulness over a few things. What a valuable lesson to learn and apply!

There is also the promise of entering into the joy of the Lord because of engaging in faithful oversight (Matthew 25:21d). As leaders, this too is very encouraging. So many things can potentially discourage us from leading others. God promises joy to those who remain faithful.

Allow me to offer this final thought. Faithfulness until the end is also an aspect of leading with fidelity. Whether the goal is completing a specific assignment, or being promoted from one responsibility to another, or departing from this world, as leaders we are to be faithful to the end (Revelation 2:10c). Our Lord Jesus was faithful until death. He was devoted to doing all His Father had sent Him to do (John 17:4). That is genuine success! We cannot obtain to perfect fidelity as our Lord did, but with that as our example it establishes the benchmark of Christian leadership.

Questions: What is your definition for leading faithfully? What is your understanding of how the Father views your current level of stewardship? What characterizes the times when you are most faithful? Least faithful?

Application: How do you stay true to the example of Christ in terms of stewardship? What steps can you take along with prayer to ensure you are faithful in all the Lord has entrusted to your care? Decide to be faithful and to finish well.

Prayer: *Father, Your faithfulness to me is so incredible and inspiring! The example of devotion demonstrated by Your Son Jesus establishes a high benchmark for me. I ask for the grace to follow His example as I seek to lead faithfully. Cause me to be more mindful to begin well and finish well because of being faithful to You. Amen.*

Day 9 - Lead with Joy

". . . always in every prayer of mine making request for you all with joy . . ." (Philippians 1:4)

For today's devotional I want to talk about joy. Paul writes to the Philippians concerning how he experienced joy as he prayed for them. His labor of love towards them was a joyous undertaking. His gratitude for them was at the root of the joy he experienced as he remembered and prayed for them. Paul is among several biblical figures who exemplify what it means to lead with joy.

In the devotional book *Sparkling Gems from the Greek,* Rick Renner writes that, "the Greek word for 'joy' is *chara* derived from the word *charis,* which is the Greek word for *grace.* This is important to note for it tells us categorically that *chara* 'joy' is produced by the *charis* ('grace') of God. This means 'joy' isn't a human-based happiness that comes and goes. Rather true 'joy' is divine in origin a fruit of the Spirit that is manifested particularly in hard times. Joy is a Spirit-given expression that flourishes best when times are strenuous, daunting, and tough." In other words, this joy is a supernatural enablement and bolsters us even in the most challenging times.

Paul's epistle to the Philippians was characterized by great joy. Although many things were occurring in his life that were not joyful, such as sitting in a dark, damp jail cell while writing this epistle, Paul maintains his joy. What an outstanding example! This joy, which is divine enablement and a fruit of the Spirit, should accompany our leading. This is one more reason to seek the Holy Spirit to be filled and refreshed daily as a leader. As we lead we must depend on His Spirit to empower us with joy as we cooperate with His will.

"The joy of the Lord is your strength" (Neh. 8:10c). God's joy provides us with strength. As we live out the things of the Lord, He graces us with His strength. I believe, based on the immediate context of that verse, His strength comes to us in the form of joy.

WORD INSIGHT

Joy (Strong's 5479) (chara) (and rejoice) is a feeling of great pleasure, of inner gladness, or of delight. Joy is an emotion evoked by a sense of well-being. It is a deep feeling of happiness and contentment. Joy in the New Testament is virtually always used to signify a feeling of "happiness" that is based on spiritual realities (independent of what "happens"). Joy is a depth of assurance and confidence that ignites a cheerful heart. It is a cheerful heart that leads to cheerful behavior. Joy is not an experience that comes from favorable circumstances but is God's gift to believers. Joy is a part of God's very essence. His Spirit manifests this supernatural joy in His children (Galatians 5:22, Acts 13:52,1 Thessalonians 1:6). Joy is the deep-down sense of well-being that abides in the heart of the person who knows all is well between himself and the Lord. (*Precept Commentary*)

Many things will come at us that have the potential to rob our joy. Sometimes, it will be people we are called to lead when we encounter unwillingness or even disobedience. Sometimes, it will be situations like getting into a car wreck or hearing a dismal health report from our doctor. But whether we are dealing with stubborn people or unwanted situations. James admonishes us to "count it all joy." Read James 1:2-3. By God's grace we can do that.

We can decide to have the joy of the Lord in difficult times. Such joy stands in contrast to the kind of happiness that is contingent upon favorable circumstances. Our joy is based on our knowledge of Jesus and knowing that He is with us no matter what we face and will take care of us and see us through. There are, of course, many and varied ways in which people and situations could diminish our joy. Yet, we are encouraged in the Scriptures to determine to be joyful.

Look at what the Word says:

- Luke 6:22, 23 – "Blessed are you when men hate you, And when they exclude you, And revile you, and cast out your name as evil, For the Son of Man's sake. Rejoice in that day and leap for joy! For indeed your reward is great in heaven, For in like manner their fathers did to the prophets."

- Acts 5:41 – "So they departed from the presence of the council, rejoicing that they were counted worthy to suffer shame for His name."

- Phillippians 2:17 – "Yes, and if I am being poured out as a drink offering on the sacrifice and service of your faith, I am glad and rejoice with you all."

- Colossians 1:24 – "I now rejoice in my sufferings for you, and fill up in my flesh what is lacking in the afflictions of Christ, for the sake of His body, which is the church."

- 1 Peter 4:13 – "but rejoice to the extent that you partake of Christ's sufferings, that when His glory is revealed, you may also be glad with exceeding joy."

But there are also times when joy will take a background role, for leading well also includes weeping with those who weep (Rom. 12:15). For instance, when a tragedy, an illness, or a death occurs godly leaders grieve with the individuals and their families.

I recall the death of our first grandson, Maximilian Alexander, who had yet to turn one year old. His sudden death rocked us all to the core of our beings. I will never forget the feeling of dealing with his passing while trying to comfort and lead my family. Seeing my son Justin and his wife, Sophie, suffering through this added to this extremely challenging time. Joy was absent, to say the least. We grieved. We were confused, hurt, and angry. To varying degrees, we still hurt even while knowing that Maximilian is in the Father's care. We all had to learn to find joy again in the Lord. It's been a journey, and we are still walking it out. But God has caused us to rejoice again. Thank you, Lord.

- "Weeping may endure for a night, but joy comes in the morning" (Psalm 30:5).

- "Those who sow in tears shall reap in joy" (Psalm 126:5).

Joy is a part of what enabled Jesus to overcome death on the Cross. It is His example we are to follow as we run our race.

- "Looking unto Jesus, the author and finisher of our faith, who for the joy that was set before Him endured the cross, despising the shame, and has sat down at the right hand of the throne of God" (Hebrews 12:2).

What was this joy that so motivated Christ? We can find the answer in Psalm 16, which expresses the faithful's confidence and the Messiah's victory. Read His expression of the anticipated joy that enabled Him to endure the Cross and despise the shame: "Therefore my heart is glad, and my glory rejoices; my flesh also will rest in hope. For You will not leave my soul in Sheol, nor will You allow Your Holy One to see corruption. You will show me the path of life; in Your presence is fullness of joy; at Your right hand are pleasures forevermore" (Ps. 16:9-11). Christ anticipated the complete joy of His Father's presence. May we, too, live and labor in anticipation of the joy of His presence.

Finally, I hope it does not need to be said that leaders will lose the joy of the Lord through sin. That can happen even with the best of leaders, as we know from what resulted from King David's sin with Bathsheba and the murder of Uriah. David lost the joy of his salvation. Psalm 51 is a stunning record of the terrible conviction he endured when the Lord called him on that sin. At some point David was able to pray: "Restore to me the joy of Your salvation and uphold me by Your generous Spirit (Ps. 51:12). Godly leaders would do well to pray regularly to keep from sin.

Every leader wants to come to a place where their leadership's fruit is accompanied by personal and heartfelt rejoicing. As John, an apostle of the Lord Jesus Christ, said: "I rejoiced greatly that I have found some of your children walking in truth, as we received commandment from the Father" (2 John 1:4). Like John, we should rejoice that those we lead are advancing in the Lord. See also Hebrews 13:17.

My prayer is that you have a new view of joy due to heeding today's devotion, and no matter where leading has found you, choose joy over everything else.

Questions: How have you defined or viewed joy? What personally has brought you joy and as a leader? What were some times or occasions when you have been tempted to abandon joy? How do you recover joy when you find that you have lost it or are losing it? What are one or two other scriptures you can add to the list we gave?

Application: Although joy is a work of grace, sometimes joy is a choice. Determine to choose joy even in difficult moments, and anticipate to rejoice again. Of the scriptures mentioned in today's devotional, which one will you use to remind yourself to anticipate or determine to lead with joy? How will you choose joy today and each day going forward?

Prayer: *Our Father, I thank You that You make joy available to Your children. I desire to choose joy every day. I pray for Your help and reminder when I am on the verge of losing the joy I have. Keep me from sin that will rob me of this joy. Please make me a person of joy. Grace me as one who leads with joy regardless of what is going in me or around me. Amen.*

Day 10 - Lead with Focus

". . . looking unto Jesus, the author and finisher of our faith, who for the joy that was set before Him endured the cross, despising the shame, and has sat down at the right hand of the throne of God." (Hebrews 12:2)

Broken focus many times leads to failure. There are potentially occasions where the Spirit of God breaks one's focus from things the Lord never intended us to pursue. But in this devotional, we are addressing those things that seek to draw our attention away from Christ and the things of Him. Those who lead well must discipline themselves to lead with focus. Leading with focus requires learning how to serve in the face of distractions. Many disrupters can and will move us off course by breaking our focus from main things. Leaders must not only be armed with this knowledge. They must also know how to keep or regain their focus each day, and they must do this amid all that is going on around them.

The writer of Hebrews admonishes us to recognize being "surrounded by so great a cloud of witnesses," who stayed focused on the Lord to eliminate those things that would break their focus. He instructs us to "lay aside every weight, and the sin which so easily ensnares us" (Hebrews 12:1). Here we are admonished to remove from us, and around us things that will distract, debilitate, disrupt, and potentially destroy us. We need God for this! But we are responsible for eradicating everything we are aware of that can cause us to lose focus.

How is "focus" defined? One aspect of the definition for "focus," given in *Webster's Dictionary,* is "directed attention." As we can see in Hebrews 12:2, the writer instructs the recipients of this epistle to make Jesus, the author and finisher of our faith. He is the One to which we direct our attention. Also "looking unto" more accurately translates as "fixing our eyes."

WORD INSIGHT

Fixing our eyes (Strong's 872) (aphorao from apo = away from something near, indicates separation + horao = look, see, behold) means to look away from all else and to look steadfastly, intently toward a distant object. The idea is to direct one's attention without distraction. The idea is putting some things away (behind) to go with a forward-gaze. This happens through inner vision (perception), persuaded about God's upcoming provision (*Precept Commentary*)

It is not enough merely to look away from that which distracts us. We must look out and focus on someone who is most worthy: the Lord Jesus Christ! He is to be our ultimate focus in life if we are to run our race successfully. Focusing on Christ does not mean not giving any attention to earthly concerns, especially those of our leadership function. No. We must make Him our primary focus, which will allow for everything else to have its proper priority in our lives and leadership. Only when He becomes the object of our obsession does everything else come into and remain in appropriate focus and perspective.

As outstanding examples, David desired one thing (Psalm 27:4), and Paul was obsessed with one thing: knowing Christ (Philippians 3:7-10). Leaders must focus, and focus on that which is worthy of their time and attention. See also Colossians 3:1-4.

One other thing. Notice that it is Jesus Christ's example of focus that is presented in Hebrews 12:2. Jesus maintained His focus by concentrating on the joy that was set before Him. His emphasis on joy enabled Him to endure the Cross and despise the shame of what His crucifixion entailed, as He apprehended and remained focused on the place He would once again occupy with His Father. Keeping the memory and experience of that joy is what kept Christ focused. Read Psalm 16:9-11. Glory to God! He was able to endure the Cross and despise the shame. Endurance is vital to maintaining our focus. Christ was not only motivated by the joy of returning to His Father's side, but He endured His earthly suffering as one who had already completed His assignment and "has sat down at the right hand of the throne of God." We are encouraged through His example to "consider him that endured such contradiction of sinners against himself, lest ye be wearied and faint in your minds" (Hebrews 12:3). Imitating Christ's focus on the joy set before

Him and the endurance working in Him is how we, too, remain focused.

WORD INSIGHT
Endured (Strong's 5278) (hupomeno from hupó = under + meno = remain) is a verb which means literally to remain under but not simply with resignation, but with a vibrant hope. It describes one who continues in an activity despite resistance and opposition. Hupomeno was used as a military term to describe an army's holding a vital position at all costs.

The noun form of **hupomeno** is **hupomone** and translates as **Perseverance** (Strong's 5281) (hupomone from hupo = under + meno = stay, remain, abide) literally means abiding under. The root idea of hupomone is to remain under some discipline, subjecting one's self to something which demands the submission of one's will to something against which one naturally would rebel. It portrays a picture of steadfastly and unflinchingly bearing up under a heavy load and describes that quality of character which does not allow one to surrender to circumstances or succumb under trial. The picture is that of steadfastness, constancy and endurance. It has in it a forward look, the ability to focus on what is beyond the current pressures (e.g., Jesus "Who for the joy set before Him endured [verb form hupomeno] the Cross despising the shame." (Precept Commentary)

For those called to lead, distractions will be plenteous. We must have the inner resolve to stay focused on what matters most and on the tasks at hand. We cannot fail in the grand scope of things if we remain focused on Jesus and according to the grace given us to the best of our ability. Leading well requires focus, a focus that looks away only to look to what matters most.

Questions: What or who tends to break your focus? Every leader must grow in self-awareness, including being aware of what distracts. As a leader, and knowing what can distract you and to what degree, how do you manage these moments? Are you focused or distracted right now? How can you tell?

Application: Knowing yourself as well as you do, and what regularly distracts you, what is your plan? How will you routinely remove or eliminate that which tends to break your focus? How will you make Christ more and more your priority and use His example of endurance to help you focus on what matters most?

Prayer: *Father, I thank You for the example of Your Son, Jesus Christ. Just as He was focused and served during distractions, I pray that You will grace me to do the same. Would you please help me identify and lay aside those things in me and about me that are weights and snares? Then, help run my race* *with my eyes looking away from that which is far less than what matters to You (Hebrews 12:1-3). Help me stay focused. Amen.*

Day 11 - Lead Wisely

"Wisdom is the principal thing; therefore get wisdom."
(Proverbs 4:7)

Leading with wisdom is about acquiring and employing the knowledge of God for a particular situation. In other words, it is about choosing God's wisdom over the insight of the world and the understanding of men. Read 1 Corinthians 1-2. This is not to say that we cannot learn from and appreciate the wisdom that may come from those who are not Christian, but it does mean knowing when that wisdom aligns with God's word. Some leaders may have trouble accepting this, but the Bible indicates that God runs the world by His wisdom and that Christians do not have a monopoly on that wisdom. Anyone may discover and apply it. Allow me to recommend as a resource for this *Uncommon Sense: God's Wisdom for our Complex and Changing World* by John Peck and Charles Strohmer.

WORD INSIGHT
Wisdom (Strong's 4678) (sophia, compare saphes = clear) is the ability to judge correctly and to follow the best course of action, based on knowledge and understanding. **Wisdom** ("God's clarity" or "God-revealed clarity") conveys the Lord's solution for problem-solving. In other words,

sophia manifests God's persuasion about solving problems or challenges by applying His solutions. Like faith, wisdom is always given by the Lord and reveals how to please Him in a particular situation. In short, this is real clarity! Ultimately all true spiritual wisdom resides in Christ, the Personification of perfect wisdom (1 Corinthians 1:30). (*Precept Commentary*)

Early on in his kingship Solomon prayed to lead God's people with wisdom. Read 1 Kings 3. A study of King Solomon's life shows many ways in which God answered his prayer for wisdom, which is a prayer to know and employ God's will in particular situations.

Solomon's insights on wisdom:

"To know wisdom and instruction, to perceive the words of understanding, to receive the instruction of wisdom, justice, judgment, and equity; to give prudence to the simple, to the young man knowledge and discretion" (Proverbs 1:2-4). "A wise man will hear and increase learning, and a man of understanding will attain wise counsel . . . The fear of the Lord is the beginning of knowledge, but fools despise wisdom and instruction" (Proverbs 1:5-7).

Here we see our need to receive the instruction of wisdom and to prove ourselves wise by hearing and increasing in learning, as well as to attain wise counsel and not be proved foolish by despising the wisdom of the Lord. Wow! In just a handful of verses, what a mighty encouragement to choose God's wisdom.

Jesus had much to say about wisdom:

- "But wisdom is justified by all her children." Luke 7:35

- "I will give you a mouth and wisdom which all your adversaries will not be able to contradict or resist." Luke 21:15

- "Therefore whoever hears these sayings of Mine, and does them, I will liken him to a wise man who built his house on the rock." Matthew 7:24

- "Behold, I send you out as sheep in the midst of wolves. Therefore be wise as serpents and harmless as doves." Matthew 10:16

- "Who then is a faithful and wise servant, whom his master made ruler over his household, to give them food in due season?" Matthew 24:25

Paul, an apostle, wrote much about the necessity of God's wisdom:

- "Therefore do not be unwise, but understand what the will of the Lord is." Ephesians 5:16

- "Oh, the depth of the riches both of the wisdom and knowledge of God! How unsearchable are His judgments and His ways past finding out!" Romans 11:33

- "that the God of our Lord Jesus Christ, the Father of glory, may give to you the spirit of wisdom and revelation in the knowledge of Him." Ephesians 1:17

- "Him we preach, warning every man and teaching every man in all wisdom, that we may present every man perfect in Christ Jesus." Colossians 1:28

Undoubtedly, you can locate many other places in both the Old and the New Testaments that speak to the need for leadership wisdom. The best wisdom, the type required to lead well, comes from above. See James 3:13, 15, 17.

I believe all of this is necessary, and summed up, in Paul's admonition that those called to build the Father's house must be wise master builders (1 Corinthians 3:10-17).

Questions: What does "leading wisely" look like to you? How do you know when you are leading with wisdom? What do you do every day to ensure that God's wisdom is the primary source that informs your leadership? How do you evaluate and employ any knowledge from the world, comparing it to the wisdom of God?

Application: Study the wisdom books of Scripture: Job, Proverbs, and Ecclesiastes. Mark the many mentions of "wisdom." Pray and develop a strategy for implementing that which you discover into your leadership function. Read one chapter from Proverbs each day for thirty-one days. What other things can you think of to improve the wisdom you possess and utilize?

Prayer: *Father, no wisdom will ever surpass Yours. I pray that You will grace me not only to be wise but to lead with wisdom that comes from You. Grant me wisdom similarly as You did Solomon, that I may live and lead well. Make me more intelligent than all my instructors. Please give me the understanding to lead well. Amen.*

Day 12 - Lead by Example

"Let no one despise your youth, but be an example to the believers in word, in conduct, in love, in spirit, in faith, in purity." (1 Timothy 4:12)

Leadership is influence by example. That is why character is so essential for leaders. In most places where the Bible lists leaders' qualifications, the requirement and criterion of godly character is given prominence over function. It is amazing how we give more credence to position and anointing than we do example or character.

Paul admonished his protégé, Timothy, to first "Be an example to the believers" (1 Timothy 4:12). After this, Paul discusses how Timothy, and others who desire to lead well, are to apply this charge. They are to be examples "in word, in conduct, in love, in spirit, in faith, in purity." The idea is to *keep on becoming* an example, to continue becoming a pattern of godly character to others. The specific expectation is that leaders become a model worthy of imitation for others.

This Greek word for "example" (tupos) properly means a "model" or "pattern" or "mold." As it applies to leadership, this word would carry the meaning of "an example to be imitated." Leaders must be examples worthy of imitation. As a result, they are also persons of influence. Leaders must steward well this vital entrustment.

WORD INSIGHT

Example (Strong's 5179) (tupos from túpto = strike, smite with repeated strokes) literally refers to a visible mark or impression made by a stroke or blow from an instrument or object. What is left after the stroke or blow is called a print, a figure or an impression. For example, the most famous reference to a literal mark (tupos) is when Thomas doubted Jesus' resurrection from the dead declaring "Unless I shall see in His hands the imprint (tupos) of the nails" (John 20:25).

Stated another way tupos properly means a "model" or "pattern" or "mold" into which clay or wax was pressed (or molds into which molten metal for castings was poured), that it might take the figure or exact shape of the mold. Our English word "type" is similar and originally referred to an impression made by a die as that which is struck.

Tupos also came to be used figuratively of a pattern, mold, model, or copy of the original of something, whether a physical object, such as a statute, or a principle or virtue. Thus in a technical sense tupos is the pattern in conformity to which a thing must be made. In an ethical sense, tupos is a dissuasive (tending to dissuade) example, a pattern of warning or an example to be imitated, the latter being Paul's obvious meaning in this verse.

Tupos was also used to identify an example or model to which one should not be conformed. For example, the children of Israel's behavior in the OT are a type which is a warning for believers today, because we will be conformed to them if we do not exercise caution. Our doom will correspond to theirs. Therefore, they stand as stern warnings to us. See 1 Corinthians 10:6, 11. (*Precept Commentary*)

Paul, writing to the Philippians, even spoke of his own life to entreat others to follow his example: "Brethren, join in following my example, and note those who so walk, as you have us for a pattern" (Philippians 3:17). See also Philippians 4:9. Every leader and aspiring leader must be mindful that many people are watching and learning from their examples. The goal is to become a pattern, a model, of godly character. Also, Philippians 3:18-19 helps us see the implications of being a poor example or pattern. None of us should desire to use our influence in that manner.

What is true of Paul should be true of those of us who are privileged to lead. In 2 Timothy 1:13 Paul counsels Timothy to retain the pattern of his teaching: "Hold fast the pattern of sound words which you have heard from me, in faith and love which are in Christ Jesus." See also 2 Timothy 3:10-15. In 1 Corinthians 11:1, Paul urges the Corinthians, "Imitate me, just as I also imitate Christ." That is the summit of leadership character, and it is a most worthy goal to attain.

In teaching citizens of the Kingdom how to live, Jesus set forth a very detailed agenda. Read Matthew 5-7.

Peter, an apostle, identified Christ as our example in all things, especially in suffering (1 Peter 2:21). The point being, the more significant the model, the more impactful the influence of our leadership.

There are numerous examples of leadership worthy of emulation. I would encourage the study of the leadership function of Moses, Joshua, David, Deborah, Esther, Lydia, and Jesus Christ. Please pay particular attention to how their example influenced the leadership of others. For instance, Moses demonstrated deep humility and dependence on

God. He knew he could not fulfill his leadership assignment without God's wisdom and help. Moses showed consistent compassion for the Lord's people. David expressed uncommon courage and a strong desire to please the Lord. He was also very zealous for the name of the Lord. David exemplifies a wise leader as he, too, was dependent on the Lord. Esther set forth her leadership example as she yielded to Mordecai's counsel and took on a daunting task that could have proven deadly for her. God uses her to stand up for her people, securing salvation for the Jews. Mordecai demonstrated godly leadership by refusing to compromise. Read Esther 3:1-6.

Barak is also a poor leadership example, especially as contrasted to Deborah. Deborah boldly steps in and accompanies Barak into battle, telling him that a woman instead of him would receive the glory for the Lord's victory. Read Judges 4-5. There are so many worthy of character study, both good and bad representations of leadership. I encourage you to make studying them one of your pursuits. Remember, leadership is influence by example.

Questions: How would you qualify your example as a leader? Is your model strengthening your influence positively or diminishing it negatively? How do you know? What do you see in Jesus' example as a leader that you need to adopt?

Application: Plan to conduct a character study on some notable leaders, paying particular attention to their character. Who will you choose? What can you take away from their example and include as an aspect of your leadership toolbox to enhance your godly influence?

Prayer: *Father, I have been made more aware today of the connection between my example and leadership influence. I pray that You make me a person of exceptional character and integrity. I desire to lead by the best standard possible. Thank You for equipping me with all that I need to be and do so every day. Amen.*

Day 13 - Lead with Understanding

"'Choose wise, understanding, and knowledgeable men from among your tribes, and I will make them heads over you.'" (Deuteronomy 1:13)

For those who aim to lead well, understanding is paramount. The word "understanding" appears over one hundred and fifty times in Scripture. The emphasis and need are difficult not to see. This word means to possess insight, intelligence, and skill. In Exodus 31:3, we see the first biblical use of "understanding." Bezalel had a certain level of artisan skill. Scripture identifies him among those who were gifted artisans. God chooses to endow Bezalel, especially by calling him to lead this team of artisans to build the Tabernacle. Moses records this in Exodus: "And I have filled him with the Spirit of God, in wisdom, in understanding, in knowledge, and in all manner of workmanship." God adds to what Bezalel already possessed.

Understanding is a quality that leaders must pursue and develop. The Book of Proverbs references understanding dozens of times. Proverbs 1:2 informs us that the purpose of Proverbs is "To know wisdom and instruction; to perceive the words of understanding." Proverbs 4:6-7 tells us, "Get wisdom, get understanding: forget it not; neither decline from the words of my mouth. Wisdom is the principal thing; therefore get wisdom: and with all thy getting get understanding." I believe the Father not only grants us understanding but that He encourages us to pursue it, to seek it, and then uses those who have sought after and acquired it. God wants us all to obtain understanding.

Those who lead must be those who have, and continue to receive, understanding from Him especially. The Lord's instruction in Deuteronomy 1:13 is for Moses to choose not only wise and knowledgeable men to have oversight of Israel's tribes but men who had an understanding or who had already demonstrated that they possessed it. Moses was feeling overwhelmed in his leadership role and asked God for help. To get the kind of help Moses needs, God instructs him to find men of understanding. Leaders need understanding, and they need those who lead along with them to be persons of understanding as well.

Solomon asked for understanding and God granted his desire. "Therefore give to Your servant an understanding heart to judge Your people, that I may discern between good and evil. For who is able to judge this great people of Yours?" (1 Kings 3:9, 11). And God answered that prayer for understanding. In writing the majority of the Proverbs, Solomon shares the importance of understanding and emphasizes this quality.

Reflect on these verses from Proverbs:

- Proverbs 2:2-3, 6 – "So that thou incline thine ear unto wisdom, and apply thine heart to understanding; Yea, if thou criest after knowledge, and liftest up thy voice for understanding; For the Lord giveth wisdom: out of his mouth cometh knowledge and understanding."

- Proverbs 3:5 – "Trust in the Lord with all your heart, And lean not on your own understanding."

- Proverbs 3:13 – "Happy is the man that findeth wisdom, and the man that getteth understanding."

- Proverbs 8:14 – "Counsel is mine, and sound wisdom: I am understanding; I have strength."

- Proverbs 9:10 – "The fear of the Lord is the beginning of wisdom: and the knowledge of the holy is understanding."

King David had men of understanding in his midst. "And of the children of Issachar, which were men that had understanding of the times, to know what Israel ought to do; the heads of them were two hundred; and all their brethren were at their commandment" (1 Chronicles 12:32).

Ezra demonstrates understanding and wisdom as he sought out men of understanding to assist in the Lord's work. "Then I sent for Eliezer, Ariel, Shemaiah, Elnathan, Jarib, Elnathan, Nathan, Zechariah, and Meshullam, leaders; also for Joiarib and Elnathan, men of understanding" (Ezra 8:16).

Paul prayed for the saints at Colossae to receive spiritual understanding: "For this reason we also, since the day we heard it, do not cease to pray for you, and to ask that you may be filled with the knowledge of His will in all wisdom and spiritual understanding" (Colossians 1:9; see also Ephesians 1:18).

Paul exhorted the saints at Ephesus to "understand what the will of the Lord is" (Ephesians 5:17). He also urged the Corinthians to be mature in understanding: "Brethren, be not children in understanding: howbeit in malice be ye children, but in understanding be men" (1 Corinthians 14:20). Understanding is crucial for those who lead.

WORD INSIGHT

In the New Testament, there are two words for **understanding** (Strong's 1271) (dianoia from dianoéomai = to agitate in mind in turn from dia = separation + noeo = to think over, nous = mind, intellect, thought, reason) means thinking through something, meditating, reflecting. It refers to the intellect, moral understanding, or the way of thinking. It is the faculty of thinking, comprehending, and reasoning. Dianoia is the seat of perception and thinking, the faculty of understanding, feeling, desiring.

Understanding (Strong's 4907) (sunesis/synesis from suniemi = to comprehend, reason out in turn derived from sun = with or together + hiemi = send) literally is a sending together or a bringing together. Sunesis describes the putting together, grasping or exhibiting quick comprehension. Sunesis is the ability to understand concepts and see relationships between them and thus describes the faculty of comprehension, intelligence, acuteness, shrewdness. It identifies people who demonstrate the ability to understand something quickly, almost intuitively. The mind that understands (suniemi) grasps concepts and sees their proper interrelationships. In the Bible this understanding speaks of the spiritual awareness of a man's heart, an awareness that can only be obtained by dependence on the Spirit of Truth Who alone can "decrypt" God's Word and guide us into all the Truth (John 16:13; 14:26). (*Precept Commentary*)

Having led in several contexts, I have grown in my appreciation of understanding as a leadership quality. For example, in doing the work of reconciliation among various Christian ethnicities, I have learned to understand the cultural differences before recommending strategies or next steps. Experience has provided me with a more in-depth understanding of this landscape and allows me to engage with those involved more knowledgeably. Understanding various perceptions, experiences, history, and so forth has enabled me to speak into these situations and help lead those involved into demonstrated unity.

As they ponder to pursue the best course of action, leaders must be those who can think something through with intellect, perception, reasoning, and comprehension. The times in which we lead are indeed uncommon. As a result, we need exceptional understanding, especially of the Lord's will, to know what we are doing. Leading well necessitates leading with understanding.

Questions: How do you seek understanding? How have you developed it over time? What has been a time where you did not lead with understanding? What did you learn from that time, and how did you adjust your leadership function as a result? If you were to encourage another to lead wisely, what would you say?

Application: Purpose to ask God for understanding every day. What additional and legitimate sources of understanding will you seek? Write out your strategy for growth in understanding.

Prayer: *Father, I ask You to grace me with supernatural understanding. I recognize how important this quality is for effective leadership. Please grant me the ability to understand concepts and see relationships between them and the faculty of comprehension, intelligence, acuteness, shrewdness. Open the eyes of my understanding. Please give me an understanding of the times in which I live and lead. Help me to lean not to my* *understanding but to seek You for Yours. I humbly ask You to make me a leader of exceptional understanding. In Jesus' strong name. Amen.*

Day 14 - Lead With Purpose

"Now My soul is troubled, and what shall I say? 'Father, save Me from this hour'? But for this purpose I came to this hour." (John 12:27)

God has given every person on the planet the common purpose to do His will. My good friend Christopher Patrick Johnson stated, "Purpose answers the question: why am I or why do I exist?" As we shall see, the Lord Jesus Christ reveals our common purpose as delighting to do the Father's will (Psalm 40:8). This is our common purpose. What was true of Christ should be true of every person on the planet.

The principle of purpose for the Christian leader comes from the Creator. It is a distinct guiding revelation every leader must know. Possessing this guiding revelation enables focus and helps avoid being distracted.

When it comes to our purpose in life and leadership, we do not define it for ourselves. Instead, we discover our God-given reason for being and leading. We do not get to determine our individual purpose or the purpose of our leadership call. The late Dr. Myles Munroe said quite often, "Ignorance of purpose makes abuse inevitable." Accordingly, if we do not take the time to discover our God-given purpose accurately, our life and leadership are futile experiments. Without a God-given revelation of our purpose in life and leadership, we can only abuse that for which we have been created.

Each of us must seek the Father for His overarching purpose for our lives, which is to obey His will. We find this in Hebrews 10:7, where we draw from the pattern of Jesus. "Then I said, 'Behold, I have come—In the volume of the book it is written of Me—To do Your will, O God.'" And in Psalm 40:8: "I delight to do Your will, O my God, And Your law is within my heart."

WORD INSIGHT

"**Will**" is the Greek word "thelema" and is the "will, not to be conceived as a demand, but as an expression or inclination of pleasure towards that which is liked, that which pleases and creates joy. Most of the New Testament uses of "thelema" (over 3/4's) refer to God's will and signify His gracious disposition toward something. The word conveys the idea of desire, even a heart's desire, for the word primarily expresses emotion instead of volition. Thus God's will is not so much God's intention, as it is His heart's desire." (*Precept Commentary*)

For those desiring to lead well, this is a goal for which to strive. Those who lead with God-given purpose for their leadership have increasing clarity regarding their life's importance and leadership's mission. I love this quote by Munroe, "Your leadership is hidden in your purpose." Chew on that for a moment!

Jesus not only knew His purpose, He attested to it: "But for this purpose I came to this hour," (John 12:27). "Purpose" here, means the ground or reason by which something is or is not done. For Christ, delight to do His Father's will was the ground or reason of His obedience. See also Luke 22:42. By understanding and embracing His purpose, Jesus could say "yes" all the way to the Cross ("this hour"). In this, Jesus is the ultimate example of Christian leadership.

In Scripture we see that Abraham, Moses, Jesus, Paul, and many other leaders knew their God-given purpose. We must realize ours today as well, specifically in our leadership function. When you see a leader, you find a person possessed by purpose. It fuels their ability to lead well.

Although we must seek God to discover our purpose, here's a word of caution. We must be careful not to mimic another person's purpose. That is not to say that there cannot be similarities. But the question is: what is it that God has uniquely purposed you to be and do? Also, keep in mind that purpose in this sense may be progressive and unfolding.

Questions: What is your God-given purpose in leadership? How did you discover it? How are you remaining true to this purpose as it pertains to life and leadership function? How might it be unfolding?

Application: Now that you have a better idea of purpose as it pertains to leadership function, what will you do daily to lead with purpose? How will you guard and progress in your purpose?

Prayer: *Father, I thank You for making known my common purpose. And I also thank You for making known to me my unique purpose. As You bring me into increased clarity and understanding, help me to do Your will. Help me choose Your will and path for me over all other life courses I might take. Thank You for the ongoing grace to fulfill Your purpose for my life and leadership function and to help others do the same. Amen.*

Day 15 Lead Within Your Limits

"We, however, will not boast beyond measure, but within the limits of the sphere which God appointed us—a sphere which especially includes you." (2 Corinthians 10:13)

Leading well requires that we do so within our limits. We need to know what those limits are and hold ourselves accountable for staying within their confines. Sometimes this requires various types of oversight to help us remain within the boundaries of our scope of leadership responsibility or authority. One of the benefits of being in submission to others is having someone to keep us going beyond our leadership limits.

Leading within our limits speaks to those limits set upon us by God and, in many cases, defined for us by others. God may use others to set the boundaries for our leadership capacity and function. We are to heed these as unto the Lord.

Jesus Christ sets the standard for leading within our God-determined boundaries. He limited Himself to the Father especially in three distinct ways.

Read these verses and take note of how Jesus described how He limited Himself.

- John 8:26 – "I have many things to say and to judge concerning you, but He who sent Me is true; and I speak to the world those things which I heard from Him."

- John 8:28 – "Then Jesus said to them, "When you lift up the Son of Man, then you will know that I am He, and that I do nothing of Myself; but as My Father taught Me, I speak these things."

- John 8:38 – "I speak what I have seen with My Father, and you do what you have seen with your father."

Jesus limited Himself to what He heard from His Father, and to what His Father taught him, and to what He had seen with His Father. His way was never to do anything of Himself but only what He heard, learned, and saw with His Father.

Read what Paul says about his limits.

2 Corinthians 10:13-16 – "We, however, will not boast beyond measure, but within the limits of the sphere which God appointed us—a sphere which especially includes you. For we are not overextending ourselves (as though our authority did not extend to you), for it was to you that we came with the gospel of Christ; not boasting of things beyond measure, that is, in other men's labors, but having hope, that as your faith is increased, we shall be greatly enlarged by you in our sphere, to preach the gospel in the regions beyond you, and not to boast in another man's sphere of accomplishment."

1. Paul, an apostle, also knew his limits and was determined to remain within them. Note several things Paul says:
2. The apostles would not boast beyond measure.
3. Whatever boasting in the Lord they did would be confined to the limits of the sphere or the measure of the measuring rule God had appointed to them. Paul had a divinely appointed field of service.
4. He knew who was included within these limits. He writes, "a sphere which especially includes you," referring to the Corinthians.
5. Apostles would not boast in others' labors or in their spheres of accomplishment.
6. Their commitment was the increase of the faith of those within their scope.

What valuable lessons for us to learn and apply as it pertains to our limits! Functioning within our limits brings more glory to God and benefits those we lead.

As the Lord distributes assignments and giftings, He does so based on ability, which is also about limits He establishes and knows that we all possess. Gift, grace, and measure come to bear as we seek to understand and function within God's boundaries for us. We must know the extent of each of these as we seek to lead without overextending ourselves. Overextension leads to underperformance, and if it is allowed to go on long enough it can very well lead to ruin.

Paul is also proof that leadership limits can and do change over time. Acts 9:30 explains that the brethren sent him to Tarsus, where he remained until Barnabas sought him (See Acts 11:25). Even though Paul was called an apostle by the Lord, he spent five to ten years in Tarsus. During this time, Paul would have learned, among many other things, how to become the leader we know him to be and what his limits were.

At Antioch, the Holy Spirit separates Paul for the work to which He had called him and sends him to it. Read Acts 13:1-3. So we can see in Paul's life how submitting to the limits of our leadership and showing ourselves faithful will always position us where God desires.

Questions: How does Christ's example of limiting Himself to the Father in three ways compare to yours? Are you aware of the limits of your leadership function? How have you overextended yourself beyond your limitations? How have you recovered? Who are those who help you remain within your limits? How will you work to function within your limits, your measure, for God's glory and the good of those you are blessed to lead?

Application: Ask the Father to clarify His limits for your leadership function. Mark the boundaries of your leadership. What accountability measures will you employ to stay within these limits and return to them if you overextend yourself?

Prayer: *Father, make clear to me the limits of my leadership function. Keep me from desiring to lead beyond my limits. Help me not to compare my leadership function to another.*

I thank You for Your placement of me. Cause me to lead well within the measure you have assigned to me for Your glory and the good of those I am blessed to lead. Amen.

Day 16 – Lead Responsibly

"Therefore take heed to yourselves and to all the flock, among which the Holy Spirit has made you overseers, to shepherd the church of God which He purchased with His own blood." (Acts 20:28)

Paul admonished the Ephesian elders to be responsible in their leadership and oversight. They were responsible to God as those who would one day give an account for their leadership. And the elders were to be responsible to one another. Paul urges them to take heed, or take care and be on guard among themselves. He was admonishing them to be responsible for providing care to one another as a team as a plurality of elders. In many cases, the Lord's people will receive no better care from the elders than these same elders provide for one another. By being responsible to one another, elders will be better stewards of the flock of God.

Those you lead are your responsibility by stewardship. Their stewardship was a Holy Spirit entrustment. The saints are precious to the Lord. Elders are to shepherd or tend and feed and guide the Church of God, which He redeemed with the blood of His Son, Jesus Christ. Every leader is placed into a position of tremendous responsibility, and they must lead in recognition of this. Accountability and stewardship come with the territory. Leading well requires leading in a trustworthy manner. When compared to Who had entrusted them with this tremendous responsibility and how it all came to be, one cannot help but be humbly amazed. So there are certain aspects of our leadership function that we cannot delegate to others.

Another definition of responsibility is "the ability to meet obligations; the act of being accountable; a duty of trust." In See 2 Chronicles 20:1-25, we read that King Jehoshaphat could have quickly reneged on his commitment to God and the people and abandoned his responsibility as king. But instead, he steps up and does what leaders who lead well do; he kept his commitment.

Another definition of being responsible is an ability always to come through, to be someone of which it can be said: "job delegated means job done." Leaders understand that in most cases, the buck stops with them. They do not blame those they lead when things do not work out as planned. So, they seek to lead responsibly, appropriately directing as required.

I like what noted leadership expert John Maxwell says about challenging times, which can reveal things about our leadership:

1. The *dropouts*: leaders who give up and fail to take responsibility.
2. The *opt-outs*: leaders who make excuses for why they are not responsible.
3. The *holdouts*: leaders who waver too long to take responsibility.
4. The *all-outs*: leaders who own the responsibility and take action.

Which type of leader are you?

The Lord Jesus Christ expressed how He had led responsibly in the following manner: "I have glorified You on the earth. I have finished the work which You have given Me to do" (John 17:4). From this, we see that accountability is a vital component of leading responsibly. "Arise! For this matter is your responsibility, but we will be with you; be courageous and act" (Ezra 10:4). Or, as Shechaniah tells Ezra, it is Ezra's responsibility to lead the assembly of people in reform. He also tells Ezra that the people are with him, so be of good courage and do what is required. Being responsible as a leader requires that one is fully aware of that which they are responsible.

Responsibility also demonstrates itself through faithfulness. "He who is faithful in what is least is faithful also in much; and he who is unjust in what is least is unjust also in much" (Luke 16:10). Notice the contrast: the steady growth in godly responsibility and the continual decline in irresponsibility. Which way will you choose?

Realizing that we must all one day give an account for our leadership, and that our labor in the Lord is never in vain, should serve as formidable motivation to cause us to endeavor to lead responsibly. See 2 Corinthians 5:10 and 1 Corinthians 15:58.

Questions: For what are you responsible? How does knowing that leadership is also stewardship influence how you lead? What improvements can you make relative to the level of your responsibility? How are you accountable to those with which you lead? What examples of leading responsibly from the life of Christ or the apostles can serve as goals for your leadership function?

Application: State what you are responsible for as a leader. Detail your intentions for being accountable to the people and things for which you are responsible.

Prayer: *Father, I understand that ultimately I am accountable to You. I also know that I am responsible for those I lead by stewardship. I also know that I am to be accountable to those I lead alongside. I ask for Your grace in becoming appropriately responsible for those I lead in word and deed. Help me guide them as one who must give an account to You. Amen.*

Day 17 – Lead and Learn

"The things which you learned and received and heard and saw in me, these do, and the God of peace will be with you." (Phillippians 4:9)

Leadership function is a learning way. It requires us to continue to learn, grow, and develop. Continuous learning is imperative to our ongoing leadership success. Every leader who embraces leadership development has this mindset: I must continue to enrich myself to continue to grow and change. Why? Because growth without change is an impossibility.

A leader who ceases learning ceases leading. Leaders must be learners, continuous learners. Leaders are not just practitioners. They are also students. They must be inclined to study about leadership and other pertinent subjects. And because people and life are multifaceted, so must be a leader's knowledge. As a result, leaders take responsibility for their learning and create opportunities to increase and enhance their skillset.

WORD INSIGHT
Learn (Strong's 3129) (manthano related to the noun mathetes = disciple, literally a learner.) has the basic meaning of directing one's mind to something and

producing an external effect. Manthano refers to teaching, learning, instructing, and discipling. Manthano means to genuinely understand and accept a teaching, to accept it as true and to apply it in one's life. It was sometimes used of acquiring a life-long habit. (*Precept Commentary*)

There are many ways in which a leader can sustain a commitment to acquire knowledge and insights, to improve and learn from others and from situations. For example, in most cases leaders are readers. They build libraries of various resources, all with a desire to continue growing and improving and helping and leading others. They read broadly and are deeply committed to expanding their base of knowledge even beyond their specific field of endeavor. For leaders desire to be as informed as possible. But there is a more pressing goal than mere accumulation of knowledge. That more superior goal is the kind of learning that is intended to advance those being led. Leaders continue to learn so that they can continue to improve their capacity to lead others well.

Apollos is an excellent example of a leader who continually learned, and whose fruit increased because of that (Acts 18:24-28). Apollos is an amazing teacher. The Lord was using him in a significant way. But we also see that Apollos was teachable even when he was already being mightily used by the Lord. Apollos had room for improvement. Leaders must remain teachable.

Keep these things in mind:

- What you learn will define who you are.
- Who you are will influence who is drawn to you.
- Who or the quality of people drawn to you will dictate the success of your leadership function.

Leaders will be left behind by the times if they make poor decisions and judgments about what is taking place under their leadership. An excellent example of this is King Nebuchadnezzar. Read Daniel 4:1-34. For a time, Nebuchadnezzar did not learn wisely from what was going on around him. He became unteachable and under judgment because he attributed all he had to his own strength and power, and because he oppressed the poor. Eventually (vv. 34-36), He would learn the ultimate lesson of all, who the Most High God is, but at a significant cost. Leaders also acquire knowledge and learn wisely from the situations and contexts around them.

Let me close today's devotional by asking you to reflect on Paul's instruction to Timothy: "Study and be eager and do your utmost to present yourself to God approved (tested by trial), a workman who has no cause to be ashamed, correctly analyzing and accurately dividing [rightly handling and skillfully teaching] the Word of Truth." (2 Timothy 2:15; *Amplified Bible*). We study to learn, to know what to be, to think, and to do. We continue to learn because what we come to know has eternal ramifications.

Questions: What have you learned, as it applies to yourself and your leadership function? How are you using these things? What have you learned this year that you did not know or understand last year? What have you determined to learn or study this year? What are some of the mistakes from which you have learned? What have you learned from past mistakes? What is your leadership learning plan?

Application: Develop a plan for annual growth in learning. Consider breaking this down into quarterly and then monthly and weekly goals and tasks. Reward yourself for maintaining your growth program. Determine what books and other resources you will read, what conferences, classes, or seminars you will attend. What are some additional ways you can continue to learn and grow?

Prayer: *Father, give me more of a mind to learn and grow. Help me have the daily and ongoing discipline to increase my knowledge base and improve how I lead. Aid me in participating in the best experiences for learning the things You know I need to carry out Your will. Amen.*

Day 18 - Lead with Others

"And He went up on the mountain and called to Him those He Himself wanted. And they came to Him. Then He appointed twelve, that they might be with Him and that He might send them out to preach, and to have power to heal sicknesses and to cast out demons."
(Mark 3:13-15)

Teamwork was very indicative of the leadership of Jesus Christ. Jesus knew He had a small window of time not only to identify but to train, develop, equip, and release them to continue His work, which they would be responsible for replicating. See Matthew 28:18-20; Acts 1:1c.

As we come to know the nature of the Godhead better and understand God's plan, we increasingly realize the imperativeness of team ministry. The Godhead is triune in nature. God the Father cooperates and works with God the Son. Jesus Christ, the Son of God, collaborates and works with the Holy Spirit. God, the Holy Spirit, cooperates and works with the Word of God. There is zero competition among the Godhead.

In the Gospels we see Christ working with His twelve disciples. In the Epistles, we see cooperation among the saints. Leaders and people working together are apparent throughout the Word of God. However, this was not always the case. Read Mark 9:33-37. Here we find Jesus rebuking and correcting the disciples concerning who would be greatest.

One of the reasons Paul wrote 1 Corinthians was to address contentions among them. Read 1 Corinthians 1:10-13. In Corinth, arrogance, haughtiness, and pride had caused an individual to set themselves above others. Yet, in the Kingdom of God, leadership is built upon humility, deferring, preferring, and referring to one another. Mutual honor and esteem are a must as it pertains to leading with others. Tremendous blessing and wisdom from the Lord are made available to those who lead well with others.

It is impossible for one person to achieve success by themselves. Teamwork is required. The relevant people need to be aligned with the vision and active in its pursuit. One person is not enough. One of the things I have overcome is the tendency as a leader to do everything myself. Instead of thinking about what individual or team of individuals I could equip, direct, and release to carry out a task, I would do it myself. I had to discover the hard way that not only was I robbing others of the opportunity for growth and service, but I was taking too much on myself. This limited (in a wrong way) actually fulfilling a vision as fully as God may have wanted, if I had included others. Like Moses, I soon learned the thing I was doing was not good for them or me. See Exodus 18. Leading well requires leading with others.

Without followers there can be no leadership function. Leading well is a team endeavor. There is an acronym for the word TEAM: Together Everyone Achieves More. There is no "I" in "team." Leadership is too vital a calling to carry out alone. It requires the right kind of help. Jethro instructed Moses to add those to the team who were "able men, such as fear God, men of truth, hating covetousness; and place such over them to be rulers of thousands, rulers of hundreds, rulers of fifties, and rulers of tens. And let them judge the people at all times. Then it will be that every great matter they shall bring to you, but every small matter they themselves shall judge. So it will be easier for you, for they will bear the burden with you. If you do this thing, and God so commands you, then you will be able to endure, and all this people will also go to their place in peace." (Exodus 18:21-23). Leadership cannot be effectuated in a vacuum because leadership function helps others become and do what they are to be and do.

Jesus always cast vision to the disciples when they were all together as a team. Doing ministry alone was never the case. He always sent them in groups. See Luke 10:1. Our enemy also knows the importance and impact of teams, so one of his chief strategies is to separate and stagnate.

Scripture reveals a team mentality to us:

- One can chase a thousand, but two can chase ten thousand.
- A threefold cord is not easily broken.
- If any two of you agree
- Wherever two or three are gathered together in my Name
- When they were on one accord

One of my favorite teamwork scriptures is Nehemiah 4:6, "So we built the wall, and the entire wall was joined together up to half its height, for the people had a mind to work." Nehemiah expresses and celebrates this milestone during the restoration project and specifies that its achievement resulted from the people working together. Leaders cannot do it all by themselves and do so at their best. A leader who accomplishes what needs to get done through the willingness and ability of others is one who leads well.

To lead well we must bring others along with us. See 2 Timothy 2:2. Paul instructs Timothy to share the things he had learned from Paul with faithful men who could share them with other faithful men. Gospel saturation is accomplished this way and requires a team effort. Someone said if you want to go fast, go by yourself, but if you're going to go far, go with others.

Questions: What makes it challenging for you to lead with others? How do you remedy taking too much on to your "leadership plate" and not allowing others to help share the burden of vision? What is your intentional plan for identifying, training, and releasing others?

Application: If you have not already developed and implemented a plan to lead with others, how will you identify, train, develop, equip, and release others? Read Proverbs 1:5, 11:14, and 15:22. Who serves as your wise counsel?

Prayer: *Father, I pray that You cause me to lead, considering what I have read and studied today. Help me to have and improve upon a plan of leading with others. Give me wisdom for leading with them and help me establish wise counsel who can also help me lead well.*

Day 19 – Lead by Faith

"But without faith it is impossible to please Him, for he who comes to God must believe that He is, and that He is a rewarder of those who diligently seek Him." (Hebrews 11:6)

Leaders must have faith. What role does faith play in your leadership? How do you apply it to achieve results in your areas of responsibility?

Where we place our faith gets us no further than the object of it. This is why our faith must be in God. For what God calls us to do is so far beyond us that it requires faith in Him to see these things achieved. A former mentor of mine said, "What God requires, requires God." And God rewards those who diligently seek Him as the only One who can do whatever must be done, and the One who can supply whatever it is that is needed. Read Hebrews 11:6. People would not turn to leaders for help if they did not believe that the leaders had the ability and capacity to do what was being asked or expected. Leaders trust in God, have confidence in Him, because He can do the impossible (Luke 1:37).

WORD INSIGHT
Faith (Strong's 4102) (pistis): Conviction, confidence, trust, belief, reliance, trustworthiness, and persuasion. In the New Testament setting, pistis is the divinely implanted

principle of inward confidence, assurance, trust, and reliance in God and all that He says. The words sometimes denote the object or content of belief (*Spirit-filled Life Bible*).

I recall a time when our congregation had outgrown our original location. We were praying for what to do next. We could not purchase any more of the land around us, so we would have to look elsewhere. My wife, Linda, and I found a potential location at least ten times the square footage of our present site. When we went to take an unofficial look at it, I was stricken with fear. For some reason, I was afraid we would not qualify for the facility. I was scared even to call the realtor to take a look inside. My wife encouraged me to at least set the appointment. I prayed, and God caused me to believe He was with us. To make a long story short, we acquired the property, and God also provided the tens of thousands of dollars we needed to prepare the building for ministry. Not only did my faith soar, but the faith of our leaders and congregation did as well. Glory to Jesus! Leaders eventually must lead by faith.

Another definition of faith is "obedience to the revealed will of God." In other words, whatever the Lord reveals, we believe it and prove it by our obedience to it. Failures in leadership are often the result of failures to believe God or take Him at His word. Make sense?

Obedience to the revealed will of God is seen in so many biblical accounts. Numbers 13 and 14 feature such an occasion. Please read both chapters in their entirety. Caleb and Joshua are leaders led by faith. Their example illustrates leadership that takes God at His word despite what others may say or feel. Having total faith in God gave Joshua and Caleb unbounded confidence when most of Israel's leaders spoke and behaved like those who had no faith. For example, when the people doubted, Caleb spoke up, "Then Caleb quieted the people before Moses, and said, 'Let us go up at once and take possession, for we are well able to overcome it'" (Numbers 13:30). Caleb's admonition was an act of faith.

There will be occasions where a leader will have to go against the grain of unbelief in order to be obedient to the Word. But for Caleb, it was God's words that carried more weight than what potentially stood in the way of frustrating God's purpose.

Leading by faith also requires the voice or language of faith. Faith has a voice, and faith speaks. It expresses what, and, more importantly, in whom it believes. Faith that "speaks" was on display through these two leaders, especially Caleb.

Resistance can result in doubt, despair, disruption, desperation, and even a desire for desertion. Read Numbers 14. But Caleb and Joshua are commended for their faith-filled leadership and example. The insurrection and unbelief of the rebels repulsed faith-filled Joshua and Caleb. Instead of siding with the unbelievers, these two faith-filled leaders rehearsed their faith in God's ability to deliver the people into what He had promised. They urged the people not to rebel against the Lord, to not allow their fear to be stronger than their faith in His ability. Read Numbers 14:6-9. Those who lead with conviction urge those they lead that the Lord is with them, so they are not to fear that which stands up and against what we believe Him to do.

Questions: Often, a team of leaders' faith inspires God's people to believe Him for what appears impossible. Can you describe a time you and at least one other stood in faith and encouraged others to have faith in God against the odds? How do you employ faith in your leadership function? Why is a strong example of faith so critical in leading others?

Application: Doubt, unbelief, and fear can be threats to a leader. How will you use the shield of faith to defend yourself? How can you employ Scripture in building your faith as a leader?

Prayer: *Father, I thank You for giving me a measure of faith. Help me function as a leader according to the proportion of faith you have blessed me to possess. As a leader, I pray that I consistently walk by faith and not by my senses that I may please You as one who believes that You not only exist but also reward those who diligently seek You. Amen.*

Day 20 - Lead with Humility

"Likewise you younger people, submit yourselves to your elders. Yes, all of you be submissive to one another, and be clothed with humility, for God resists the proud, But gives grace to the humble." (1 Peter 5:5)

"Take My yoke upon you and learn from Me, for I am gentle and lowly in heart, and you will find rest for your souls." (Matthew 11:29)

Why would humility be considered vital to leading well? Is humility something that immediately comes to mind when you think of a godly leader? Many may view humility as being exceptionally low on the list. But it should be at the very top! As an essential quality for leadership function, it was the standout quality of Christ's leadership (Philippians 2:5-8) and that of so many that followed Him in Scripture. Therefore, it should be a priority quality for those desiring to lead well. But what is humility?

WORD INSIGHT

Greek scholar Kenneth Wuest writes of **humility** (tapeinos) in this manner, "The word is found in an early secular document where it speaks of the Nile River in its low stage. In other words, "It runs low." The word means "not rising far from the ground." It describes the Christian who follows in the humble and lowly steps of his Lord."

"**Humble**" (Strong's 5011) (tapeinos) means low, not high, not rising far from the ground. It speaks of one's condition as lowly or of low degree. It described what was considered base, common, unfit, and having little value. It pictures one brought low, as for example, by grief. Tapeinos is descriptive, particularly of attitude and social positions. (*Precept Commentary*)

These definitions should cause us as leaders to examine ourselves in terms of whether we walk humbly before God and men, as did Jesus. Would God and man say we are clothed in true humility?

The idea that God would choose to use us ought to be enough to humble the best of us.

Consider these biblical testimonies of leaders who understood this:

- Genesis 32:9-10 – "I am not worthy of the least of all the mercies and of all the truth which You have shown Your servant; for I crossed over this Jordan with my staff, and now I have become two companies."

- Exodus 3:11 – "But Moses said to God, 'Who am I that I should go to Pharaoh, and that I should bring the children of Israel out of Egypt?'

- 1 Chronicles 17:16 – "Then King David went in and sat before the Lord; and he said: 'Who am I, O Lord God? And what is my house, that You have brought me this far?'

- Psalm 8:4 – "What is man that You are mindful of him, and the son of man that You visit him?"

- Ephesians 3:8 – "To me, who am less than the least of all the saints, this grace was given, that I should preach among the Gentiles the unsearchable riches of Christ."

And there are countless others who, at the prospect of being used of the Lord, made themselves low physically and proclaimed their unworthiness for His call. Examples of such leadership include William Joseph Seymour, the African-American Holiness preacher who initiated the Azusa Street Revival, which significantly influenced the Pentecostal and Charismatic Movements. Other worthy examples would consist of Frederick Douglas, William Wilberforce, Charles Harrison Mason, Howard Thurman, Rosa Parks, Dr. Martin Luther King, Jr., and Mother Theresa. Lowliness is the posture of those who lead well, those who have put on humility, and who continue to allow the Lord to humble them so He can use them.

Pride has no place in life or leadership. God said that even a proud look is out of bounds (Proverbs 6:17). He has set Himself against the proud (James 4:6). But the Scripture teaches that He gives grace to the humble. Hallelujah! The teaching of Scripture is that we all, beginning with leaders, should "be clothed with humility." See also Colossians 3:12.

WORD INSIGHT

Clothe or Put on (Strong's 1746) (enduo) means to put on as a garment and in the middle voice (as in this verse) means to clothe oneself. The aorist imperative calls for immediate, even urgent, effective action. All believers (plural) are to do this now. (*Precept Commentary*)

I can personally attest that the problem with pride is that we may not be aware that we are walking in it, versus humility being our clothing. I recall when I walked into a Bible College class I was about to teach, and one of the students said about me, "If the Lord can save him, he can save anybody." I will never forget how I felt at that moment. I was embarrassed. I was upset. I was bothered because of who I thought I had become. Here I was, the professor of this class filled with potential ordination candidates, but someone who knew me before I was born again made this simple statement that revealed haughtiness in my heart. Christ exposed pride in me with just a few words. The Lord has used moments like those to humble me and to keep me humble. We must be on the lookout for personal pride. We must do all we can not to get lifted within ourselves, thinking more highly of ourselves than we out to think (Romans 12:3). May the Lord cause us to think soberly concerning ourselves and others.

We also need to guard against false humility. False humility looks and sounds just like true humility. False humility is very deceptive because, in most cases, we know what to say and how to behave to meet most people's expectations. Jesus used a parable in Luke 18:9-14 to illustrate false humility. "False humility is prideful. It's bragging of being humble, using the claim to manipulate or control. It seeks attention and admiration, like the Pharisees who prayed loudly on the street corners so people would know how righteous they were", writes Geraldine Fisher. I define false humility as an insidious counterfeit quality of genuine graciousness, lowliness, and meekness. Paul identified specific traits of those who practiced false humility. Read Colossians 2:18-23. Please seek to be genuinely humble, avoid pride, and shun false humility.

Consider these verses that urge us to lead with humility:

- Psalm 15:33 – "The fear of the LORD is the instruction of wisdom, And before honor is humility."
- 2 Timothy 2:24-25 – "And a servant of the Lord must not quarrel but be gentle to all, able to teach, patient, in humility correcting those who are in opposition, if God perhaps will grant them repentance, so that they may know the truth."

- Titus 3:1-2 – "Remind them to be subject to rulers and authorities, to obey, to be ready for every good work, to speak evil of no one, to be peaceable, gentle, showing all humility to all men."

There you have it! Scriptural evidence urging you to examine yourself to learn whether you are consistently leading with humility. It is not enough just to teach this to others and expect this out of them. Godly, faith-filled leaders must first manifest in reality the humility we see in the Lord Jesus, that it may be visible to others.

Questions: How have you defined humility? What are your triggers for pride and false humility? How do you avoid becoming arrogant and haughty? Has pride or false humility been an issue for you, and how do you plan to overcome and eradicate these things?

Application: Identify one or two of the scriptures provided in today's devotion that you will commit to memory. When you are tempted by pride, use these verses as the Sword of the Spirit against pride. Which ones did you choose?

Prayer: *Father, according to Your Word, I ask You to humble me and keep me humble. I know that there is no other way and, in my flesh and myself, I will never choose and remain clothed in humility. I ask for Your grace and help in Jesus' name. Amen.*

Day 21 - Lead with Conviction

"Now faith is the assurance of things hoped for, the conviction of things not seen."
(Hebrews 11:1)

The entirety of Hebrews 11 provides us with many examples of people who led with conviction. God Himself convinces them, and they thought, felt, behaved, and spoke like it. Both named and nameless individuals were so convinced of the Lord that they stood on their convictions and risked it all.

People who claim to be convinced about something have faith in it. The most remarkable object for faith and our beliefs is God. That is what Hebrews 11 teaches us. Faith in God gave these people the courage of their convictions (see Day 23).

In general, they expressed their conviction by declaring, "I know" or "I believe." They led from the courage of their faith in the One who they knew was mightier than they. They are, as Hebrews 12:1 puts it, our "great cloud of witnesses," biblical examples of leading with conviction. They show us that we too can lead in full assurance of the God who has called us and in His desire, ability, and provision to accomplish all He says or pleases.

WORD INSIGHT

This word, **Conviction** (Strong's 4136) (assurance) (plerophoria from pleres = full+ phero = bear or carry), is literally "complete carrying" and indicates entire confidence or full assurance, suggesting that one has a more substantial guarantee than the sense conveyed by the word "certainty" by itself. (*Precept Commentary*)

Verses that express conviction or full assurance relative to the things of God:

- Colossians 2:2 – "that their hearts may be encouraged, having been knit together in love, and attaining to all the wealth that comes from the full assurance of understanding, resulting in a true knowledge of God's mystery, that is, Christ Himself."

- Hebrews 6:11 – "And we desire that each one of you show the same diligence so as to realize the full assurance of hope until the end."

- Hebrews 10:22 – "let us draw near with a sincere heart in full assurance of faith, having our hearts sprinkled clean from an evil conscience and our bodies washed with pure water."

Leaders throughout the Word of God expressed their convictions relative to God. They declared their beliefs concerning who He is, what He said, and what they believed He would do. A mindset and posture like this are consistent with those who lead with conviction. Their convictions direct them, and above all other things they influence who they are, what they believe, and what they say.

Recall our working definition for leadership: *leadership is influence by example.* Therefore, leaders must lead by the right convictions, and these will have a significant impact on what those who follow them become, think, and do. An absence of reasonable belief in our leadership function will prove detrimental among those we are privileged to lead. Biblical examples of those whose model of conviction influenced others include Moses, Joshua, Deborah, David, Daniel, Esther, the three Hebrew boys, Josiah, and of course the Lord Jesus Christ.

Paul was a man of steadfast conviction. He was utterly convinced relative to the Father and of the things of the Father. In Romans 8:38, Paul expressed that he was confident of God's everlasting love: "For I am persuaded that neither death nor life, nor angels nor principalities nor powers, nor things present nor things to come." The meaning of "persuaded" in this verse is "[to convince by argument, whether something is true or false]." Read Romans 8:31-39.

Paul was convinced that nothing in this litany of things he articulates could separate him, and us by implication, from the love of God in Christ Jesus our Lord. You ought to stop and praise the Lord right here!

Consistent confidence about our convictions will be non-negotiable for those of us who intend to lead well. And we know no one comparable to our God from which to gain such ongoing assurance. I urge you to prayerfully establish accurate beliefs in the Lord and be led by them. Amen?

Questions: How have your convictions influenced your leadership over the years? What is your view of how your beliefs influence your example and the effectiveness of your leadership function? What is your strongest conviction as it pertains to your leadership role?

Application: State your undergirding convictions about life and leadership. What is your plan to establish and enhance your beliefs? How will you identify areas of opportunity for growth and change?

Prayer: *Lord, make me a leader of proper convictions. Make me lead from my primary belief of Your sovereignty. Make me a leader whose convictions correctly and positively influence others to be as convinced, and more, as I am of You and all about You. Strengthen the beliefs I currently possess and make me a model and a testimony to others. Amen.*

Day 22 - Lead in Excellence

"Then this Daniel distinguished himself above the governors and satraps, because an excellent spirit was in him; and the king gave thought to setting him over the whole realm." (Daniel 6:3)

". . . know His will, and approve the things that are excellent . . ." (Romans 2:18)

Daniel is our example here. He was a man of outstanding excellence. Specifically, he was distinguished among others because an excellent spirit was in him.

WORD INSIGHT
Webster's Dictionary defines **excellence** as the state of being exceptionally good in quality and character. The root word of excellence is "excel," which is defined as more excellent or surpassing others. Henceforth, to be a person of excellence is to surpass others by being exceptionally good in quality and character.
Excellence or Surpassing greatness (Strong's 5236) (huperbole from huperballo = a throwing beyond the usual

mark from huper = above + ballo = cast) is literally a "throwing beyond" and thus refers to a degree which exceeds extraordinarily a point on an implied or overt scale of extent. It means extraordinary, far more, much greater, to a far greater degree, surpassing, beyond measure, utterly. (*Precept Commentary*)

As a man of God, Daniel had the mind of God, a mentality to do all things well in recognition of who he represented, which was God. This "attitude of excellence" propelled him to live a cut above those who did not know God.

Daniel's godly character and unwavering stance concerning his faith in God led him to be preferred over more tenured leaders. King Darius did not pick Daniel out of the crowd because of his good looks or connections. Darius recognized Daniel's excellent spirit and publicly proclaimed Daniel's promotion even when others seemed more qualified.

Leaders who have become excellent have several distinguishing characteristics. Here are ten observations I have made that will help you become exceptional at who you are and what you do.

Ten observations of those who lead with excellence

1. Leaders of excellence are realistic and honest with themselves and others about who they are and where they are in terms of their character and abilities, and then they seek to raise the bar for all.
2. Leaders of excellence recognize mediocrity and stagnation as enemies.
3. Leaders of excellence identify and eradicate potential threats to their character and service.
4. Leaders of excellence do not strive for perfection but aim to arrive close to it.
5. Leaders of excellence endeavor to excel in the short and long term.
6. Leaders of excellence consistently engage in personal growth and improvement.
7. Leaders of excellence are mindful of how they carry themselves, so as to endeavor not to say or do anything to misrepresent the Lord Jesus Christ.
8. Leaders of excellence require excellence in themselves and others.
9. Leaders of excellence are, through example, individuals of influence.
10. Leaders of excellence are drawn to excellence.

As a leader, when you live in excellence, it will establish and exemplify a standard that followers will witness and can seek to attain. Here is how Paul, an apostle, speaks of the standard of ministry excellence set by the team of leaders who accompanied him to Thessalonica, and how that influenced the saints there: "And you became followers of us and of the Lord, having received the word in much affliction, with joy of the Holy Spirit, so that you became examples to all in Macedonia and Achaia who believe. For from you the word of the Lord has sounded forth, not only in Macedonia and Achaia, but also in every place. Your faith toward God has gone out, so that we do not need to say anything."

Paul and his leadership team's example of excellence was so profound that it influenced an entire region with the values, beliefs, and truths of the Kingdom of God. An entire region was modeling an excellent spirit. That's pretty remarkable. Read 1 Thessalonians 1-2:12 for the full context. Those who lead from an excellent spirit will have a significant impact on others. Do not take this lightly!

Here is an outstanding recommendation found in a teaching article by leadership expert Sam Chand:

"Let me provide for you a few thoughts to help you create an excellent spirit. Apply the following lists to your daily tasks. They will help separate you from those who just want to "get by." People, who are "stuck" in life, do the exact opposite of the list below.

Write the following list down and store them in a place where you visit often:

- Do not accept mediocrity!
- Make people feel important.

- A negative attitude cancels out all positive skills.
- Remember that little things make a big difference.
- Tell people how much you appreciate them.
- Under promise. Overperform.
- Never be too busy to work hard.
- Grade yourself after every performance or workday.
- Always be honest with yourself.
- People rarely forget excellent ministry service.
- Stay away from people with bad attitudes.
- Emulate people of excellence.
- Image is reality.
- First impressions are lasting.
- Expect excellence from yourself and others.
- Don't just talk about it, do it!
- When a mistake is made, correct it immediately.
- Read, study, listen and then communicate.
- Do the simple things in an excellent way.
- Excellence is not an option.
- Be excellent at all times. Everyone is watching.

The above phrases sound simple, but if you meditate on them and apply them to your daily tasks, promotion is headed your way!" (*"A Few Excellent Thoughts to Help You Stand Out"*)

Questions: What made Daniel such a person of excellence? What does this imply concerning what is required to be such a person? Why and how should this be true of your leadership function? Do you work hard to improve yourself continuously? How do you feel after a late or mediocre delivery of your service? Do you find ways to improve your next opportunity or simply accept complacency? What threatens your excellence? Procrastination? Disorganization? Overeating? Lack of exercise? Lack of knowledge?

Application: Determine to upgrade everything that is not excellent. In other words, work on yourself. Challenge mediocrity in your life and among those who you lead. Get rid of any perceived or actual threats to excellence. Develop new relationships that inspire excellence in you. Develop a long-term strategy recognizing that excellence demands our preparation.

Prayer: *Father, according to Psalm 8, Your name is excellent. I pray as You live in me that I more and more exemplify the spirit of excellence that is consistent with Your name. Make me a person of excellence and cause me to bring You much glory and positively influence Your people that they endeavor to live this way.*

Day 23 - Lead With Courage

"Be strong and of good courage, for to this people you shall divide as an inheritance the land which I swore to their fathers to give them." (Joshua 1:6)

Joshua is one of the more notable leaders in the Bible and one of my personal favorites. His display of leadership function teaches us so much. The Lord speaks to Joshua (Joshua 1:6) as He commissions him for service. Joshua was about to assume the leadership function after Moses, who must be in the Universal Hall of Fame of Leaders (I made that up; to my knowledge, nothing like this exists). Undertaking that responsibility must have been a very daunting task. God knew that and so He urged Joshua to be strong and of good courage. We, too, must see this, because courage originates from what we confidently know.

Winston Churchill called courage the first human quality because it is the quality that guarantees all others. Franklin Roosevelt said, "Courage is not the absence of fear, but rather the assessment that something else is more important than fear." A variation of this says, "Courage is not the absence of fear but the ability to act in spite of it." Courage is a requirement for those who lead well.

Joshua had to know that God was with him, as this would be the source of his courage. The Lord stresses this in Joshua 1:2-5. Especially notice verse 5: "No man shall be able to stand before you all the days of your life; as I was with Moses, so I will be with you. I will not leave you nor forsake you." These words would instill courage in Joshua, especially as he recalled how God had been with Moses. God's promise to Joshua of His presence, power, and provision gave Joshua the ability to take and maintain courage. From God's promises, Joshua is to lead Israel into the land the Lord promised. His convictions about God fueled his courage in God (Day 21). Joshua 1:5 was also an implied warning that these people would give him with ample opportunities not to be a strong, courageous leader. Joshua would need the help of the Lord to be consistently brave. Notably, those who would lead along with Joshua expected him to be courageous. Listen to their declaration, "Whoever rebels against your command and does not heed your words, in all that you command him, shall be put to death. Only be strong and of good courage" (Joshua 1:18).

WORD INSIGHT
The first scriptural mention of the word "**courage**" is found in Numbers 13:20, where it means "to strengthen, prevail, harden, be strong, become strong, be courageous, be firm, grow firm, be resolute." The admonition or exhortation to be of "good courage" is found throughout scripture. It also tends to be accompanied by a call to also "be strong" (Strong's). In the New Testament, **courage** (Strong's 2292) (tharrheo from thársos = boldness) means to display or have

courage, an attitude of confidence or firmness of purpose in face of danger or testing. be courageous, have courage, be bold, be of good cheer. "To have certainty in a matter." (*Precept Commentary*)

Some passages about courage:

- Deuteronomy 31:6-7 – "Be strong and of good courage, do not fear nor be afraid of them; for the Lord your God, He is the One who goes with you. He will not leave you nor forsake you." Then Moses called Joshua and said to him in the sight of all Israel, "Be strong and of good courage, for you must go with this people to the land which the Lord has sworn to their fathers to give them, and you shall cause them to inherit it."

- Joshua 1:9 – "Have I not commanded you? Be strong and of good courage; do not be afraid, nor be dismayed, for the Lord your God is with you wherever you go."

- 1 Chronicles 28:20 – "And David said to his son Solomon, "Be strong and of good courage, and do it; do not fear nor be dismayed, for the Lord God—my God—will be with you. He will not leave you nor forsake you, until you have finished all the work for the service of the house of the Lord."

- 2 Chronicles 15:8 – "And when Asa heard these words and the prophecy of Oded the prophet, he took courage, and removed the abominable idols from all the land of Judah and Benjamin and from the cities which he had taken in the mountains of Ephraim; and he restored the altar of the Lord that was before the vestibule of the Lord."

- Ezra 10:4 – "Arise, for this matter is your responsibility. We also are with you. Be of good courage, and do it."

- Acts 28:15 – "And from there, when the brethren heard about us, they came to meet us as far as Appii Forum and Three Inns. When Paul saw them, he thanked God and took courage."

Paying close attention to these verses, we see that strength is somehow connected or required to being of good courage. There is no more necessary courage than what God supplies. Those who rely on Him and trust His promises have what it takes to be of good courage. What this at times requires is that we act even when we face fearful circumstances. Even amid uncertainty or fear, courageous actions strengthen our leadership function and inspire the same in those we lead.

Leaders who lack courage will find it challenging to inspire others. King Saul is a picture of what happens when a leader lacks courage. See 1 Samuel 10:17-15:14.

In his book, *21 Indispensable Qualities of a Leader*, leadership expert John Maxwell writes about King Saul's negative example of courage as a leader and its impact. He writes: "Courage and cowardice are both contagious. Without courage, it does not matter how good your intentions are. Only courage allows you to do what you are afraid of doing. Without courage, we are slaves of our insecurity and possessiveness. If the leader lacks courage, the people will lack commitment (1 Samuel 15:24). A leader without courage will never let go of the familiar (1Samuel 28:5-20). Lack of courage will eventually sabotage a leader (1 Samuel 31:1-6)." Leaders who lack courage will not lead well and maybe not for very long.

Those we lead need our example of courage to help supplement their courage, especially in the execution of vision. Read 1 Samuel 30. Verse 6 shares with us that despite how David felt and what he was going through, he encouraged himself (KJV), strengthened himself, in the Lord.

WORD INSIGHT
Encourage (*Strong's* H2388) means "to fasten upon; hence, to seize, be strong (figuratively, courageous, causatively strengthen, cure, help, repair, fortify)." (*Precept Commentary*)

We must recognize that David was encouraged in the Lord. The Lord's encouragement was not a fleshly pep talk. The result was that David led two hundred men against tremendous odds, to recover everything that had been stolen from them. Courage has also been defined as the capacity not to be regulated or hindered by fear or uncertainty. In other words, courage is the effective management of challenge or uncertainty. David's example surfaces a principle and a pattern for us as we desire to lead with courage. Through this narrative we see that God is the source of our encouragement, the motivation to act on our courage.

Elijah the prophet is another excellent example of leading with courage. Read 1 Kings 18:1-40. Elijah's courage motivated him to overcome his misgivings, his doubts, and his complaints.

By now, you should see how vital courage is to leadership function. I pray that today's devotion encourages you to lead with the courage you have.

Questions: How courageous are you? What is generally the source of your courage? Have there been times where you did not demonstrate courage as a leader? Why was this the case, and what did you learn? How have you prepared yourself so that this is not the case in the future? Can those around you attest to your courageousness? How can you increase your courage?

Application: Do what you can to discover what you do not know about those fearful matters you face. Where possible, acquire the skill needed to deal with what lies before you. Plan to partner with others who may be equally or more courageous than you. Stop dreaming about acting. Make a plan and do it. Where there is uncertainty, work with what you know. Do your part and trust God with His portion. Exercise the courage you do possess often.

Prayer: *Heavenly Father, I thank You that You supply all that we need, especially when we need it. You know that as a leader I require courage. I pray that all the courage I need will be in me each time I need it. Your will requires it. Make me a person of courage and cause me to take courage to lead Your people into what You promised. Amen.*

Day 24 – Lead With Compassion

"But when He saw the multitudes, He was moved with compassion for them, because they were weary and scattered, like sheep having no shepherd." (Matthew 9:36)

If there were ever one leader who could serve as the poster personality for compassion, it would be the Lord Jesus Christ. He is the epitome of the compassionate leader. Jesus' entire life was a life of compassion. If you want to learn to lead with compassion, Jesus is your one-stop example.

The late Dr. Adrian Rogers once said that - Jesus looked at the marching, milling multitudes on their way to Hell and wept tears over them. "He was moved with compassion"—not just that He had compassion; *"he was moved with compassion."* His heart caused Him to act.

The word compassion in Matthew 9:36 means to suffer. It also means "from the pit of your stomach." The Latin word for compassion means "to suffer with." In Latin it is a very powerful word; it literally means "to convulse; convulsed."

What good is orthodoxy without compassion? What good is it to dot every "I" and cross every "T" if we can't spell the word compassion? Someone has well said, "People really don't care how much we know until they know how much we care." Jesus felt compassion for them. Here, we see the real heart of Jesus, for His ultimate mission was to seek and save the lost (Luke 19:10, Mark 10:4+). As He encountered the depth of their depravity and their monumental need, He was moved with compassion. Jesus felt sympathy with and for the people. He took pity on them.

We should never think of Jesus as unfeeling or stoic in the face of people's problems, and this same truth applies today. He is still filled with deep compassion for His creatures. When we have compassion, we learn to suffer with other people. No man has ever been a faithful man of God, and no man has ever been a devoted deacon (servant-leader) until he's a man of compassion. Is Jesus not a powerful example of leading with compassion?

WORD INSIGHT
In Matthew 9:36, this phrase is actually "**Felt compassion** (Strong's 4697) (splanchnizomai from splagchnon = bowel, viscera) and means to experience a deep visceral feeling for someone, to feel compassion for, to feel sympathy, to take pity on someone. *Splanchnizomai* is the strongest word for pity and describes the compassion which moves a man to the deepest depths of his being. Compassion is the sympathetic consciousness of others' distress together with a desire to alleviate it. This verb expresses an outward

flow of one's life in contrast to our natural tendency toward self-centeredness. It is not surprising that eight out of twelve New Testament uses describe this deep-seated emotion in Jesus. It follows that if we desire to imitate Jesus, we need to be men and women of deep compassion!" (*Precept Commentary*)

Gospel passages depicting Jesus' compassion:

- Matthew 14:14 – "And when Jesus went out He saw a great multitude; and He was moved with compassion for them, and healed their sick."

- Matthew 15:32 – "Now Jesus called His disciples to Himself and said, 'I have compassion on the multitude, because they have now continued with Me three days and have nothing to eat. And I do not want to send them away hungry, lest they faint on the way.'"

- Matthew 20:34 – "So Jesus had compassion and touched their eyes. And immediately their eyes received sight, and they followed Him."

- Mark 1:41 – "Then Jesus, moved with compassion, stretched out His hand and touched him, and said to him, "I am willing; be cleansed."

- Mark 5:19 – "However, Jesus did not permit him, but said to him, "Go home to your friends, and tell them what great things the Lord has done for you, and how He has had compassion on you."

- Mark 6:34 – "And Jesus, when He came out, saw a great multitude and was moved with compassion for them, **because** they were like sheep not having a shepherd. So He began to teach them many things."

- Mark 8:2 – "I have compassion on the multitude, because they have now continued with Me three days and have nothing to eat."

- Luke 7:13 – "When the Lord saw her, He had compassion on her and said to her, 'Do not weep.'"

If compassion moved the Lord Jesus Christ to serve and lead, how can any of us who resolve to lead well not do the same? It is this kind of leadership that transforms lives and changes the world!

Questions: How has this devotion spoken to you? What is it about Jesus' example of compassionate leadership that speaks to you most? Have you considered how compassion is so integral to leadership function? Why does compassionate leadership play such a vital role in leading anyone?

Application: Listen to what others are saying. Truly listen. Be mindful of those with whom you are engaging. Cultivate empathy for those you serve and lead. Determine to help make people's lives better. Seek to be more understanding. Practice patience and genuine interest. Always accept and give quality feedback. Keep in mind that how you engage and treat people is typically the byproduct of the value you place on them. Your level of compassion for them is the result of how you truly see them.

Prayer: *Father, as Your servant I desire to serve and lead Your people with compassion. Fill my heart with compassion similar to the compassion that so moved Christ for others. You gave us the Model Example in Your Son Jesus. Help me to be others'-minded as He was. Help me to see others through Your eyes and to love and treat them as He would. Amen.*

Day 25 - Lead With Decisiveness

"Go, gather together all the Jews that are present in Shushan, and fast ye for me, and neither eat nor drink three days, night or day: I also and my maidens will fast likewise; and so will I go in unto the king, which is not according to the law: and if I perish, I perish." (Esther 4:16)

Decisiveness is the ability to study various situations and circumstances presented to us and then make sound decisions without fear. This includes a willingness to fail rather than avoid responsibility. Leaders must be decisive.

Queen Esther demonstrates decisiveness in her leadership function. Read Esther 2-4. She was forced to make a life or death decision that would impact not only her life but many other lives. Esther is hesitant to involve herself at the direction of her uncle Mordecai. But she relents after Mordecai sends an additional response to explain what was on the line (Esther 4:10-14).

She chooses to be decisive and steps into action, requesting her people and her staff's support. That is what it means to lead with decisiveness. Those who rely on the wisdom of the Lord are more inclined to be decisive.

Christ was decisive. What enabled Him to be so was His relationship with and confidence in the Father. This confidence was derived from His intimate and unique knowledge of the Father. As a result, and being one who did nothing of Himself, He limited Himself to what He heard from the Father, had been taught by the Father, and had seen alongside the Father (John 8:26, 28, 38). I believe this is what made Jesus a decisive leader. He was utterly Father-centered and Father-reliant. Many leaders are indecisive because they lack this type of relationship, which results in a lack of confidence in the Father and what He desires to do through them.

Decisive leadership needs wise decision-making skills. Even after gathering the necessary information, weighing the facts, and counseling with credible others in prayer, leaders must decide the best course of action. Because their decisions have implications in others' lives, leaders must decide, or choose, wisely.

Those who lead decisively:

- Keep God completely and entirely involved in the process, being consciously aware of His sovereignty, desiring that His will be done.
- Know that the decisions they make will influence the quality of the decisions made by others.
- Are mindful that their decisions will potentially have a long-term impact.
- Welcome the counsel of others but know the decision is yours to make.

Decisiveness also speaks of those who, except the Holy Spirit leads otherwise, stick with their decisions, do not question them, or waver in them. Of course, there are times where leaders make decisions that appear appropriate but are later determined to be wrong. Even when leaders are confident their decision is the proper one, they can realize that a decision needs to be amended, revised, or even repented when wisely questioned. Leaders must decide to make corrections in instances such as these. So I am not talking about indecisiveness which can cause an environment of instability. Those we lead have a right to expect us to be decisive in our leadership function. Where we are decisive, vision can be advanced. Where we are indecisive, vision can be deterred or derailed. Leaders must learn how to make quality decisions each day.

There will be times when the options are many but a clear-cut choice is not readily visible. At times like this, a leader must have some basis for determining what will constitute quality and godly decisions. For example, various entities often seek our local assembly to either lead or partner in multiple efforts that benefit our city, but our desire to serve our city and region must be kept in check as we weigh the various options for involvement. During the COVID-19 pandemic, we were asked to serve meals to families twice per week for a specified period. Needless to say, as things worsened with the pandemic the need for food distribution increased. As the demand increased, our capacity to continue this ministry was strained. Our elders' team had to make a decision. We were presented with the options of securing more volunteers, or cutting the distribution to one time per week, or eliminating the program. We chose to cut the delivery to one time per week. This allowed us to continue to serve our city while being mindful of those faithful volunteers who supported this vital program. Many principles guided our decision: our dedication to God's glory, prayer, the impact this would have on those serving, consistency of this effort with our overarching vision, and a commitment to make decisions as a team.

The following three questions should be answered to qualify an excellent and godly decision, especially when the choice is unclear.

- Will this bring God glory or misrepresent Who He is?
- Will this positively affect the people we are leading?
- Does this choice fit into God's overarching purpose or His subordinate purposes?

If you can answer yes to all three, I believe you are well on your way to making a proper decision and leading decisively as a result.

Questions: What has been your tendency where decisive action is required? Who are your go-to people, along with the Father, when a significant decision must be made? Are you decisive or indecisive? What would others say, and why? What are you doing, or what have you done to improve your decision-making ability? How can you utilize the three decision-making questions above or some variation to help you make better decisions?

Application: Learn from your past decision-making efforts. Know that you are not infallible, but that God is. Realize that not making a decision is making one. Make decisions from the proper disposition. Be honest about your motivations and intentions. The most informed decisions are predominately bathed in prayer and with wise counsel. Define your criteria for success. Make effective decisions, not necessarily comfortable ones. Own your choices. They are yours.

Prayer: *Father, I desire to be as decisive as You and Your Son. So I pray that You would grant me the grace to make wise, sound, godly decisions bathed in prayer and with wise counsel. I pray that none of my choices are fundamentally selfish. May they all be for Your glory, within the confines of Your purpose, and with significant consideration of all those who are involved. May I have the patience to wait on Your leading and guidance. May I hear Your voice and follow You. I pray and ask all of this in Jesus' name. Amen.*

Day 26 – Lead With the End in Mind

"He said, 'It is finished!" (John 19:30)

"The end of a thing is better than its beginning . . . " (Ecclesiastes 7:8a)

The end of a thing can and does mean many things. It could be moving from one role to the next. It could include being promoted to an increased level of leadership and responsibility. It could be leaving one area of assignment for a completely different field of endeavor. It should include planning to leave the people and the places that have been impacted by your leadership function more competent, developed, and capable than they were before they engaged with you.

Scripture teaches us that our ultimate ambition is to be well-pleasing to our Lord (2 Corinthians 5:9). This ambition should drive us as it pertains to a particular project, mission, assignment, or role, and ultimately the end of this earthly life.

Leadership function will require carrying out many and various projects, missions, assignments, or roles. Leading well means giving strong consideration to completing any of these in light of what is expected of us, and most of all to the pleasure of our Lord.

Jesus spoke of the importance of finishing projects in Luke 14:28-33. He provides two clear examples to the multitudes following Him. The first example is about building a tower and the necessity of sitting down first and counting the cost to know whether one beginning a project of this magnitude has enough to finish it. Jesus' second example speaks of a king going to make war against another king, and how the attacking king must sit down first and consider whether he has the necessary troops to defeat the enemy. In either instance, not finishing brings dire consequences, as well as being mocked for not achieving the desired end, and having to compromise for something relatively less significant. The point is that leaders must get started, put in the appropriate thought, and strategize, and then work towards the desired end.

Dr. Stephen R. Covey wrote, "Your most important work is always ahead of you, never behind you." As a growing leader, this statement really impacted how I chose to view my leadership journey. Early in my leadership development, I remember reading and seeking to implement what I read in Covey's now-classic book, *The 7 Habits of Highly Effective People*. He detailed the second habit in this highly informative book is "Begin with the end in mind." The fundamental idea of this habit is to help those who lead to focus. A quote from his website states that to "Begin with the end in mind" is a personal mission statement that "focuses on what you want to be and do. It is your plan for success. It reaffirms who you are, puts your goals in focus, and moves your ideas into the real world." I like Covey's thought, here, but for the Christian leader the principle would focus on the Lord Jesus Christ.

I borrowed and adjusted a definition of "success" for my life from one of my mentors, the late Otis Lockett, Sr. Here is what I have determined: "success is knowing God, (how He defines success or the successful), what He wills and desires for my life, growing to my maximum potential in the Lord, and sowing seeds that will benefit others in the advancement of Christ's Kingdom." To lead well means to focus on what Jesus wants a leader to be and do. That should be your plan for a humble and godly leadership function. It affirms who Jesus is (your Lord!) and puts His goals in your sights, and it moves His purposes through into the real world. As servants of the Lord, we should desire to hear, "Well done good and faithful servant; you were faithful over a few things, I will make you ruler over many things. Enter into the joy of your Lord" (Matthew 25:21).

Every task, every project, every assignment, every role should include this type of thinking. I believe the key to ultimately finishing well is what we do along the way. In the Parable of the Talents (Matthew 25:14-30), Jesus makes it clear that those who are found faithful in the Lord's eyes are those who demonstrate faithfulness over a few things. In this Parable there was a point of completion, where three individuals were evaluated based upon a predetermined outcome. Most of what we do as leaders consist of a few things we must manage well based on a predetermined outcome. Leading with the end in mind requires us to assume this posture in our ministry or work. Since we have no idea how what we are stewarding or leading right now will impact our near or distant future, we must develop a penchant for not only starting but finishing well. And if the goal is to achieve the desired end and be well-pleasing to the Lord, the rest should take care of itself.

The Lord Jesus Christ led with the end in mind. He knew how His life would end here on earth. But most importantly, He knew what awaited Him when His earthly existence would come to an end. He knew that He was destined to return to the place He had eternally and uniquely been, which was with the Father (John 1:1, 14, 18). Knowing this should help us to see that Jesus led with the end in mind.

Leading with the end in mind requires that we have insight into what the Father desires us to do. This is what we want to finish, while all the while seeking to bring glory to Him. Jesus is, again, our example: "I have glorified You on the earth. I have finished the work which You have given Me to do" (John 17:4). And Jesus cried, 'It is finished'" (John 19:30). He could only utter this if He were keenly aware of what "finished" entailed.

WORD INSIGHT
This word for "**finished**" (John 17:4) in the Greek is (Strong's 5048) teleioō from G5046 teleios; to complete, i.e. (literally) accomplish, or (figuratively) consummate (in character): —consecrate, finish, fulfill, make) perfect. The root of this word is teleios from telos = an end, a purpose, an aim, a goal) means complete, mature, fully developed, full-grown, brought to its end, finished, wanting nothing necessary to completeness, in good working order. John

19:30, on the other hand, is the Greek word, teleō (Strong's 5056), which translates as "to end, i.e., complete, execute, conclude, discharge (a debt):—accomplish, make an end, expire, fill up, finish, go over, pay, perform." (*Precept Commentary*)

Both of these words and their corresponding definitions help us comprehend what Jesus models in His leadership function: He knew what the end looked like. He was fully aware of what it would require and entail. He knew who He was and what work He must do to be able to say to His Father, "I have finished the work which You have given Me to do." Notice Christ says that the work He finished was "given" to Him by the Father to do. "Given" means, in this case, "to give to one's care, entrust, commit; something to be administered" (*Thayer's Greek Lexicon*). Our Lord understood the specific work He was given to administer. In John 4:34, in response to His disciples' concern over whether He had eaten, Jesus replied, "My food is to do the will of Him who sent Me, and to finish His work." In other words, Jesus was given, or entrusted with, a stewardship by His Father. His work was His Father's eternal aim. He had been given to care for that which the Father eternally desired. Read John 17:1-5.

At a minimum, I hope today's devotion helps you ponder whether you lead with the end in mind. One thing we know is that Jesus left behind successors. We cannot lead well if our success is not evidenced in what we leave behind.

Questions: What is the work that the Father has entrusted to you to finish? What has He ordained for you to complete within your lifetime or for a specific people or place or role? Do you have a written, up-to-date personal mission statement? What is your exit strategy for your current role? How will you know when it is time to depart and what must be done before leaving? Have you identified and prepared a successor?

Application: Spend some concentrated time in prayer around what you are uniquely called to be and do. Write down and keep updated on your mission statement. With each assignment, be sure you know what you are to complete before you can say, "It is finished."

Prayer: *Father, help me clearly know who you desire me to be and what it is You have called me to do. I also ask that You help me to discern when it is time for me to move on to whatever You have next for me. With each leadership function experience, help me understand and do what You have entrusted me to be. Please make me a person who desires to demonstrate goodness and faithfulness and do well what you expect of me. Amen.*

Day 27 - Lead Knowing God is Your Father

"All things have been delivered to Me by My Father, and no one knows the Son except the Father. Nor does anyone know the Father except the Son, and the one to whom the Son wills to reveal Him." (Matthew 11:27)

How can knowing God is my Father assist me in being the leader I am called to be? For the Believer who has been given leadership function, knowing God as Father has several vital implications.

Ephesians 1:3-14, which is one long sentence in Greek, is Paul's proclamation of why God the Father is to be "blessed" (spoken well of in extravagant terms) by His sons and daughters. The Father is to be because He has lavished us with everything through His Son, Jesus Christ. Not one spiritual blessing is denied us. We understand that His adoption of us makes these benefits available to us. Note that adoption is listed among these.

Just in these verses alone, we find a litany of benefits we receive as His sons and daughters:

1. Election (v. 4) – His sons and daughters are chosen by the Father, for the Father, and unto the Father, before the world began to be holy, without blame, before Him in love.
2. Predestination (v. 5) – As His sons and daughters, we have a predetermined destiny.

3. Adoption (v. 5) - We are supernaturally made His family.
4. Sonship (v. 5) - His sons and daughters receive the full rights, privileges, and responsibilities of sonship.
5. Destined to the praise of His glorious grace (v. 6, 12) - Our adoption as His children ultimately reverberates to His glory.
6. Acceptance in the Beloved (v. 6) - As the Father is forever pleased with His Beloved Son, we who are in Christ are forever accepted by the Father.
7. Redemption (v. 7) - The blood of Christ has secured our redemption, liberation, salvation, and deliverance according to the riches of His grace.
8. Forgiveness (v. 7) - Remission/forgiveness of our sins is ours through Christ's blood.
9. Access to the wealth of His grace (v. 7-8) - What God has done for us in Christ makes available to us the riches and the generosity of His gracious favor, which abounds to us in all divine wisdom and understanding.
10. He granted us the revelation of His will (v. 9) - He unveils the mystery of His will to us according to His purposed good pleasure.
11. He made known to us his internal purpose in Christ (v. 10) - The idea here is "the heading-up-again of all things in Christ" and the superintending of those things in heaven and on earth.
12. He revealed to us that we were made to be His inheritance (v. 11) - The Amplified Bible sums up the

benefit we receive here most appropriately, "In Him we also were made [God's] heritage (portion) and we obtained an inheritance; for we had been foreordained (chosen and appointed beforehand) in accordance with His purpose, Who works out everything in agreement with the counsel and design of His own will."

13. Destined and appointed to live for the praise of His glory (v. 12) – As those who have trusted in Him, He has destined our lives to be ever praiseworthy of Him.
14. Sealed with the Holy Spirit (v. 13-14) – We are "authorized" and sealed as with the Holy Spirit of promise as His purchased possession, all for His glory.
15. Promised glorification (v. 14) – Our sonship's "future" tense is the promise here. One day we will actually inherit the "unfathomable riches of Christ (Ephesians 3:8), "an inheritance which is incorruptible and undefiled and that does not fade away, reserved in heaven for" us (1 Peter 1:4). The Holy Spirit is the guarantee and down payment of our inheritance.

Take a moment and worship the Lord for just these few benefits of being His child.

Knowing God as your Father enables you to serve Him as a son or a daughter and not a spiritual orphan. Generally, spiritual orphans are laden with identity issues. They commonly have no idea who they are, why they are, or where they are going. Their person is frequently tied to their performance. They often draw their worth, value, and significance from what they do instead of who they are to the Father and in Jesus Christ. Regularly they seek to prove themselves through their performance to people and to God, failing to appreciate and accept how the Father values and accepts them and what God has already so lavishly given them.

Be reminded of what He has given to those who are His sons/daughters. Summarily, the Father has given us His approval, acceptance, assurance, acquittal, and abundance. Glory to Jesus! Those who do not know Him operate from an orphan mind and heart. They generally think, believe, feel, and act as those who are entirely on their own! More often than not, orphans have little to no protection and no provision beyond what they can generate for themselves as they tend to struggle to survive by any means necessary. In particular, as a son to the Father, one endowed with leadership function, protection, and provision is a part of being in the Father's house. Sons to the Father comprehend that the Kingdom of God's culture is that of a household, and in His family, we are supplied all we will ever need (Ephesians 2:19).

Jesus, the Pattern Son, knew this like no one else. He already knew the Father's approval and acceptance before He did one thing of note, according to Luke 1:32. Matthew 3:17 does not discount this, as some view Jesus' obedience in baptism as the motivation for the Father's approval where Matthew records, "And suddenly a voice came from heaven, saying, "This is My beloved Son, in whom I am well pleased." God the Father spoke aloud what Jesus Christ, the

Son, had eternally known, which was that the Father had already approved and accepted Him, and it had nothing to do with Christ's performance. Amen to that.

So many Christians who lead are driven by so many things instead of resting in this profound truth. Instead, their leadership is characterized by the need to perform, impress, be recognized, and even belong to something other than the household of God. Well, if you belong to the family of God, God is your Father, too! And that means you do not have to live one more moment seeking to perform for anyone or belong to some group. You don't have to strive to impress anyone or be recognized by anyone or belong to anything. You no longer have to do any of this because you already belong to that which matters most, and that is the household of God!

Another powerful benefit of knowing that God is your Father is that you do not have to concern yourself with living as if you are your own source. See John 5:30a. The leadership lifestyle Jesus modeled was one where He lived with the Father as His only Source. Who Jesus was while here on earth, what He did, and what He said had their genesis with the Father.

Reflect on these verses:

- John 4:34 – "Jesus said to them, "My food is to do the will of Him who sent Me, and to finish His work."
- John 5:30 – "I can of Myself do nothing. As I hear, I judge; and My judgment is righteous, because I do

not seek My own will but the will of the Father who sent Me."

- John 6:38 – "For I have come down from heaven, not to do My own will, but the will of Him who sent Me."

- John 8:26 – "I have many things to say and to judge concerning you, but He who sent Me is true; and I speak to the world those things which I heard from Him."

- John 8:28 – "Then Jesus said to them, "When you lift up the Son of Man, then you will know that I am He, and that I do nothing of Myself; but as My Father taught Me, I speak these things."

- John 8:29 – "And He who sent Me is with Me. The Father has not left Me alone, for I always do those things that please Him."

- John 8:38 – "I speak what I have seen with My Father, and you do what you have seen with your father."

These verses reveal and establish a pattern that we should embrace as we seek to lead, as did the Lord Jesus Christ. How He thought, felt, believed, and acted came from His relationship with His Father. A disposition such as this must be the case for each of us. Let's press deeper into it.

Jesus not only knew that God was His Father, but He was also secure in this reality and truth. Knowing this secured Jesus in His ultimate identity, purpose, and destiny.

Knowing this meant that the business He was ultimately about was His Father's business. He understood that He came to reveal His Father to men.

WORD INSIGHT
"Know" (Strong's 1921) (epiginosko [Epiginōskō] from epí means upon but is used here to intensify the force of the following verb + ginosko = to know) (See related noun epignosis) means to know fully, to know with certainty, to become thoroughly acquainted with or to know thoroughly, exactly, fully, or completely. Epiginosko means to possess more or less definite information about and can imply a degree of thoroughness. It speaks of full or added knowledge. To be fully acquainted in a discerning, recognizing manner. (*Precept Commentary*)

Experiential knowledge such as this defines how Jesus knew that God was His Father. And it is how He derived this full, thorough, and accurate knowledge, which is also the place of genesis for His ministry as a servant-leader. The Lord Jesus Christ Himself is the archetype servant-minster.

Where did He derive this knowledge, and how was this the place of initiation and sustaining for His leadership function? It was borne out of a profound, personal, steadfast, believing, and a face-to-face relationship with His Father (John 1:1-18). This relationship consistently defined and directed His leadership. He was able to lead and finish well, completing what had been uniquely assigned to Him as the result. If you desire your knowledge and relationship to be anywhere near what Jesus had in terms of its quality, you to must determine to know the Father as did Christ. Knowing God as Father in and of itself will help you to lead and lead well beyond what you could have ever imagined.

Questions: What are your immediate thoughts after reading today's devotion? How do you view God? Do you see Him as Father? How does the manner in which Jesus knew and related to the Father now affect how you will determine to know and relate to Him? What adjustments do you need to make regarding how you think, feel, believe, and act? Has your relationship as a leader been to the Father? How are you relating to Him in light of the benefits of your sonship?

Application: Meditate on the verses from the Gospel of John. Identify what adjustments you need to make to follow Jesus' pattern as a Son who led knowing His Father.

Prayer: *Father, after today's devotion, Your name takes on a whole new meaning for me. I pray to know You fully,* *thoroughly, and accurately. Help me to no longer do or say anything of myself. You are my Source. I am Your son, and I am not a spiritual orphan. I thank You that protection and provision are made available to me as a member of Your household. I never have to perform again for men or You. I receive Your approval, acceptance, assurance, acquittal, and abundance. In Jesus' strong name. Amen.*

Day 28 - Lead After the Example of Christ as Son

"And He who sent Me is with Me. The Father has not left Me alone, for I always do those things that please Him."
(John 8:29)

In the previous devotion we reflected on what it means to lead well by knowing God is your Father, and Jesus was our example for that. Directly related to that, of course, is Jesus as the Son of the Father. In today's devotion I want to focus on what it means to lead well by following the example of Jesus as the Son.

We know and believe that all three Persons of the Trinity, God the Father, God the Son, and God the Holy Spirit, are all equal in essence and that these, being one God, are equal in deity, power, and glory. However, in John 8:29, we see that the Lord Jesus Christ is fully submitted to the Father, although equal in nature. John writes: "And He who sent Me is with Me. The Father has not left Me alone, for I always do those things that please Him." Notice that Jesus' testimony is that He always does that which pleases the Father. His example of submission is a model for all those who lead. Another example of Jesus' submission to His Father is seen in His willingness to be sent by the Father to serve as our Savior. John writes in his epistle, "In this is love, not that we loved God, but that He loved us and sent His Son to be the propitiation for our sins" (1 John 4:10).

The Lord Jesus also knew that the One who sent Him was also "*with*" Him. "And He who sent Me is with Me" further compounds the Father's abiding presence and their uncanny relationship as Christ carried out the work His Father had sent Him to do. What a fantastic confidence booster to leaders, especially in times of distress. God the Father never left Jesus except in that moment on the Cross when Jesus said, "My God, My God, why have You forsaken Me?" (Matthew 27:46). Yet after saying "I thirst" (John 19:28) and "It is finished" (John 19:30), the Lord Jesus proclaimed, "Father, into thy hands I commit My spirit" (Luke 23:46). Amazing! He was declaring His return to the Father - full circle.

During Jesus' earthly sojourn He never lost this relational connection and vital intimacy with the Father except that one time. Jesus' example is a tremendous model for those who lead and have been sent by the Father to abide in Him and to be one with Him. Jesus described this abiding presence as He and His Father being one. He exclaimed, "I and My Father are one" (John 10:30). We, too, must abide in Him. Read John 15:1-8.

Note, too, that the Son never sends the Father. These roles or functions are never reversed in the Word of God. It is the Son who perfectly submitted His will to the Father's will (Luke 22:42; Heb. 10:7).

"Jesus said to them, "My food is to do the will of Him who sent Me, and to finish His work" (John 4:34). This verse reflects another aspect of leading after the example of Christ as the Son. What was essential and lifegiving to Jesus was "to do the will of Him who sent (Him) and to finish His work." As the Son of the Father, Jesus knew His unique purpose was to do the Father's will. Hebrews 10:7 (see also Psalm 40:6-8) speaks to this, "Then I said, Behold, I have come—In the volume of the book it is written of Me—To do Your will, O God." Doing the Father's will was Christ's purpose and delight. His mind was set on accomplishing the will of His Father. The Son was committed and delighted to do His Father's will.

As we lead, no matter the sphere of our leadership, we seek to accomplish the Father's will and not our own. His intention is to be known by us and to become our singular delight. Christ was eternally obligated not merely to do His Father's will but also to finish it. We, too, must be committed to completing the work the Father has sent us to do. I hope you are following this pattern.

For Christ, it was God the Father who had His back, fully supporting and advancing all He sent Jesus to do. This is leadership function at its finest! Even those who express their leadership function in the marketplace should see themselves as being sent and backed by the Father. As a result, you know to Whom you have submitted your will. In your marketplace context, you represent the One who sent you, so take confidence in what this means and affords you.

The Lord Jesus Christ and the Father were so much "one" that Jesus could say things such as this: "though you do not believe Me, believe the works, that you may know and believe that the Father is in Me, and I in Him" (John 10:38; see also John 14:10, 11). Our job, too, is His work.

Take a few moments to reflect on these statements Jesus made:

- "I can of Myself do nothing. As I hear, I judge; and My judgment is righteous, because I do not seek My own will but the will of the Father who sent Me." (John 5:30)

- "For I have come down from heaven, not to do My own will, but the will of Him who sent Me." (John 6:38)

We also have Jesus' words in John 8:29: "The Father has not left Me alone, for I always do those things that please Him." Jesus knows in carrying out the Father's will, He is never alone. How magnificent is that? What an example we have in Him!

Please ponder this and measure your leadership function alongside His.

Questions: What has this devotion spoken to you? How have you been leading as did Christ led, as we shared above? How have you not been leading as Christ did? Explain why it is so critical to have God the Father with you and in back of you. How significant is it that you know and consistently desire to do the Father's will and why should you do so? As one with leadership function, to whom is your will submitted? Who is it who has sent you? In other words, who and what is the origin of and authority behind your leadership function?

Application: Take some time and pray through the verses above, noting where you need to make changes in your leadership function to be more aligned with Christ's. What steps will you take to make this a consistent part of how you lead? Who will help hold you accountable so that you lead well in this area as did Christ?

Prayer: *Father, thank You for opening my eyes and allowing me to see the remarkable example of Your Son, the Lord Jesus Christ. Please make me more like Him, not just in leadership but in life. May I be one who is devoted to Your purpose for me, which is doing Your will. Thank You that You not only sent me but that You are also with me, in back of me, that you will never leave, and You are committed to helping me do those things that are pleasing to You. Amen.*

Day 29 - Lead Being Led by the Holy Spirit

"For as many as are led by the Spirit of God, these are sons of God." (Romans 8:14)

In today's devotion, we intend to look at why it is critical to be led by the Holy Spirit. The Holy Spirit, on many occasions, is the forgotten member of the Trinity. Yet we know and understand that He is equal in essence, deity, power, and glory to God the Father and God the Son. The Father sent the Holy Spirit to the Church so we could continue to "both do and teach" all that Jesus began (Acts 1:1).

In Christ, the archetype servant-leader, we see the Father's workings in and through a life for His glory. Christ was not only filled with the Holy Spirit (Luke 4:1), but led by the Spirit: "Then Jesus was led up by the Spirit into the wilderness to be tempted by the devil" (Matthew 4:1).

WORD INSIGHT
"**Led**" is the Greek word, "an-ag'-o"; from Strong's G303 and G71; to lead up; by extension to bring out; specially, to sail away:—bring (again, forth, up again), depart, launch (forth), lead (up), loose, offer, sail, set forth, take up. Depicted here is how surrendered Jesus was to the

Father's will. This word for "led" was often used to illustrate creatures that were led by a rope tied around their necks. Once tied to that rope, these creatures willfully followed wherever their master led them. (*Precept Commentary*)

Christ's tenure here on earth was under the leadership of the Holy Spirit, because to be filled with the Spirit is to be under the Spirit's influence, leadership, and control. In being led by the Spirit even into testing, Jesus exemplified how leading well requires that we are guided.

WORD INSIGHT

"**Be filled**" (Strong's 4137) (pleroo) means literally to be filled to the brim (a net, Mt 13:48, a building, Jn 12:3, Acts 2:2, a city, Acts 5:28), and then figuratively to make complete in every particular, to cause to abound, to furnish or supply liberally, to diffuse throughout, to pervade, to take possession of and so to ultimately to control. The more common figurative meaning of filled in the NT is to be controlled by that which "fills" one's heart and mind.

(*Precept Commentary*)

What was true of Christ and must also be true of us. It behooves us to know that the destination(s) and ultimate destiny God has for our lives has one Guide: the Holy Ghost. Read what Jesus spoke to His disciples, "However, when He, the Spirit of truth, has come, He will guide you into all truth; for He will not speak on His own authority, but whatever He hears He will speak; and He will tell you things to come. He will glorify Me, for He will take of what is Mine and declare it to you" (John 16:13, 14).

Pay close attention to the following verses:

- Acts 10:19 – "While Peter thought about the vision, the Spirit said to him, "Behold, three men are seeking you."

- Acts 11:12 – "Then the Spirit told me to go with them, doubting nothing. Moreover these six brethren accompanied me, and we entered the man's house."

- Acts 13:2-4 – "As they ministered to the Lord and fasted, the Holy Spirit said, "Now separate to Me Barnabas and Saul for the work to which I have called them. Then, having fasted and prayed, and laid hands on them, they sent them away. So, being sent out by the Holy Spirit, they went down to Seleucia, and from there they sailed to Cyprus."

- Acts 16:7 – "After they had come to Mysia, they tried to go into Bithynia, but the Spirit did not permit them."

- Acts 20:28 – "Therefore take heed to yourselves and to all the flock, among which the Holy Spirit has made you overseers, to shepherd the church of God which He purchased with His own blood."

In each verse mentioned, we can see the Holy Spirit's leadership and control. His leadership and influence are irrefutable requirements for those who want to lead well. They must be those who lead after the Holy Spirit. And along the way, it is who they are becoming under the Spirit's influence that matters most. I often say, "On your way somewhere, become somebody."

Also, and quite importantly, the Holy Spirit is not only leading us to do specific tasks or to go to certain places. He is leading us to a Person. I believe that teaching apostle and author the late DeVern Fromke captures this best, as he wrote concerning Romans 8:14-17.

Fromke writes in *The Ultimate Intention*, "God's intended pathway for Adam was sonship (Romans 8:16; 1 John 3:2, 3 Amp.), heirship (Romans 8:17; Ephesians 4:13) and throneship (Romans 8:17; 2 Timothy 2:12). But these three phases of God's plan can only become real as His sons learn to be led by the Spirit, *"For as many as are led by the Spirit of God, they are (mature) sons of God"* (Romans 8:14). From eternity, God's call to Adam and his posterity has been to enter into sonship, which is the gateway to:

- PARTICIPATION – in His very life and purpose
- APPROPRIATION – of all that God desires to share
- QUALIFICATION – by discipline for the throne (end of quote)

The Holy Spirit is leading us to the Person of God's Son, so that we are conformed to the image of His Son (Romans 8:29). Conformity to Christ's Person is our most significant destination. Conformity to His image is where we are being led. This transformation occurs as we follow the leading of the Holy Spirit.

Being led by the Spirit requires that we heed Paul's command: "I say then: Walk in the Spirit, and you shall not fulfill the lust of the flesh" (Galatians 5:16). Kenneth Wuest translates the verse: "But I say, through the instrumentality of the Spirit habitually order your manner of life, and you will in no wise execute the passionate desire of the evil nature" (*Word Studies in the New Testament Greek, Volume One*). Our life and leadership is to be habitually ordered by the Holy Spirit.

Those privileged with leadership function need to be led. Just as the Spirit led the Lord Jesus, we too must yield to the Spirit's leading and guidance. Our submission to Him is vital. It benefits us and those we lead. May the Holy Spirit become your preoccupation as He leads you.

Questions: Why should it matter to you as a leader who it is you follow daily? How would you rate your submission to the leadership of the Holy Spirit? Why is it impossible to lead well if the Holy Spirit is not the Guide? How have you made the Holy Spirit your preoccupation?

Application: Study Romans 8 and make notes which you will apply to your leadership. Pay particular attention to how God is utilizing His Spirit to bring you to His appointed end. How do you determine to ensure that the Holy Spirit habitually orders your life and leadership?

Prayer: *Lord, teach me how to follow the Holy Spirit as a leader of people. I know that You are leading and guiding me through Him. I open my heart to Him that He may direct me where it is You desire. Father teach me to recognize the Spirit's voice and realize what He is leading me to be and do. Make me more receptive to the Holy Spirit so that He can lead me in the path You have ordained for me. Amen.*

Day 30 - Lead Yourself

"For I say, through the grace given to me, to everyone who is among you, not to think of himself more highly than he ought to think, but to think soberly, as God has dealt to each one a measure of faith." (Romans 12:3)

Leading well begins with leading yourself. Leading yourself is self-government. And by this, I do not mean things such as self-centeredness or loosening the reins on the flesh. The Bible condemns such things. Instead, I mean matters such as self-discipline and self-control. I like the way Dr. Tony Evans puts it: "Self-government means control of one's attitudes and actions apart from external coercion. Self-government is the foundation for leadership and every other form of government since those who cannot govern themselves cannot properly govern others. God's ultimate goal for humanity is self-government under Him".

How can you lead others well if you first do not lead yourself well? Remember: leadership is godly influence by Christ-like example. How well you lead yourself is fundamental to your example and influence. Leading yourself is about character, integrity, self-awareness, personal growth, and development. It is about self-discipline and self-control. It is comprised of having and maintaining an accurate view and understanding of who you are, why you are, and where you are going. Leading yourself well requires that you keep your heart's motivations, desires, and ambitions in check and allow the Spirit of God to dictate them.

It also consists of individual commitments and nonnegotiables you establish for yourself. Reflect on how much Paul, an apostle, wrote to his spiritual sons and fellow apostles, Timothy and Titus, concerning this:

- 1 Timothy 4:12-16 – "Let no one despise your youth, but be an example to the believers in word, in conduct, in love, in spirit, in faith, in purity. Till I come, give attention to reading, to exhortation, to doctrine. Do not neglect the gift that is in you, which was given to you by prophecy with the laying on of the hands of the eldership. Meditate on these things; give yourself entirely to them, that your progress may be evident to all. Take heed to yourself and to the doctrine. Continue in them, for in doing this you will save both yourself and those who hear you."

- 2 Timothy 1:6-7 – "Therefore I remind you to stir up the gift of God which is in you through the laying on of my hands. For God has not given us a spirit of fear, but of power and of love and of a sound mind."

- 2 Timothy 2:1, 3-7 – "You therefore, my son, be strong in the grace that is in Christ Jesus. You therefore must endure hardship as a good soldier of Jesus Christ. No one engaged in warfare entangles himself with the affairs of this life, that he may please him who enlisted him as a soldier. And also if anyone competes in athletics, he is not crowned unless he competes according to the rules. The hardworking farmer must be first to partake of the crops. Consider what I say, and may the Lord give you understanding in all things."

- 2 Timothy 2:15 – "Be diligent to present yourself approved to God, a worker who does not need to be ashamed, rightly dividing the word of truth. But shun profane and idle babblings, for they will increase to more ungodliness."

- 2 Timothy 2:20-21 – "But in a great house there are not only vessels of gold and silver, but also of wood and clay, some for honor and some for dishonor. Therefore if anyone cleanses himself from the latter, he will be a vessel for honor, sanctified and useful for the Master, prepared for every good work."

- 2 Timothy 2:22 – "Flee also youthful lusts; but pursue righteousness, faith, love, peace with those who call on the Lord out of a pure heart."

- 2 Timothy 2:23-26 – "But avoid foolish and ignorant disputes, knowing that they generate strife. And a servant of the Lord must not quarrel but be gentle to all, able to teach, in humility correcting those who are in opposition, if God perhaps will grant them repentance, so that they may know the truth, and that they may come to their senses and escape the snare of the devil, having been taken captive by him to do his will."

- Titus 2:12 – "teaching us that, denying ungodliness and worldly lusts, we should live soberly, righteously, and godly in the present age."

In these and many other verses Paul is calling leaders to a Jesus-like form of self-government. In his, *Five Teachings of Grace* (*Forerunners Commentary*), John W. Ritenbaugh calls it self-mastery. He wrote, "Self-mastery . . . is self-government or self-control, the foundation of strong godly life, growth, and producing fruit. If a person cannot govern himself, if he cannot master his passions, he will certainly not have a good relationship with his fellow man or God. His life will likely be marked by significant excesses.

"The biblical writers use this word in various ways: to behave in an orderly manner, be sober, grave, sane, sound-minded, discreet, self-disciplined, prudent, and moderate. In the context of a person controlling himself, Paul writes, 'For I say, through the grace given to me, to everyone who is among you, not to think of himself more highly than he ought to think, but to think soberly, as God has dealt to each one a measure of faith' (Romans 12:3; see Titus 2:6; I Peter 4:7).

"A person who has self-mastery is even-handed, and his passions are under control. He makes proper use of his drives and desires, and his manner of life is not one of extremes. A person reflecting this quality will be making steady progress in growing into the perfectly balanced character of Jesus Christ." Ritenbaugh provides outstanding instruction for leaders here.

Paul kept himself under control while admonishing his readers to a similar pattern.

"Do you not know that those who run in a race all run, but one receives the prize? Run in such a way that you may obtain it. And everyone who competes for the prize is temperate in all things. Now they do it to obtain a perishable crown, but we for an imperishable crown. Therefore I run thus: not with uncertainty. Thus I fight: not as one who beats the air. But I discipline my body and bring it into subjection, lest, when I have preached to others, I myself should become disqualified" (1 Corinthians 9:24-27).

These verses offer a good word for all leaders.

My friend Jonathan Leath has written an excellent book entitled *YOLO: You Only Lead One*. In it he gives eight principles for leading yourself before you lead others. I encourage you to add it to your leadership library. Jonathan, who is an outstanding leader of leaders, writes about "A-N-A-B-O-L-I-C" leaders. He says exceptional leaders demonstrate these qualities:

A=Authentic,
N=Nice,
A=Accurate,
B=Brilliant,
O=Objective and Open-minded,
L=Lead with Love,
I=Integrated, and
C=Character.

He explains these principles and encourages leaders to develop them as evidence of "a solid personal leadership foundation."

I agree with Jonathan Leath and encourage you to build your own list. Identify where you need to put the necessary focus and then work so that who you are and who you are becoming allows you to be a leader who is worthy of being followed (1 Corinthians 11:1).

Questions: What person, biblical or otherwise, would you use as a model for someone who, under the leadership of the Holy Spirit and the Word of God, led themselves well? Please state why or what about them made you choose this particular individual. How do you hold yourself accountable and ensure that you lead yourself better than you lead others?

Application: Build a list of qualities and next steps you need to engage with as you lead yourself routinely. Identify where you need to put the necessary focus and work, so that who you are and who you are becoming allows you to be a leader who is worthy of following.

Prayer: *Lord, I know that leading myself is foundational to all other leadership functions I provide. So I ask You to assist me in leading myself very well. Help me to see myself through Your eyes. Make me honest with myself, my strengths, weaknesses, and areas for growth. I not only want to continue to be a person of character, honesty, and integrity, but I also desire to be someone who is self-disciplined and practices self-mastery. May I become more sensitive to the Holy Spirit as it pertains to my leadership of me and consistently become the person You have envisioned. Amen.*

Day 31 - Lead as a Servant

"And He sat down, called the twelve, and said to them, "If anyone desires to be first, he shall be last of all and servant of all." (Mark 9:35)

We have arrived at our final day in this 31-Day Leadership Development Devotional. Where has the time gone? This last entry is a culmination of the things you delved into in the other thirty days. This time of investment was about one thing, encouraging you to lead well.

I made this commitment to you early on as I articulated my purpose for writing this book. This is what I said: "My purpose in writing this Leadership Development Devotional is to encourage and inspire 'growing' leaders to lead well as they continue in their leadership journey." That's right! Leadership and its function is a journey. It is not a destination. Leadership is also a stewardship. We will all give an account of how well we have led. And those of us gifted, entrusted, and called to lead must have a consistent mentality to lead well. We measure our leading well by standards determined by the God who has graced us to lead. And He equates leadership with servanthood.

I want to leave you with one final challenge. I want to strongly encourage you to lead as a servant of the Lord. In the final analysis, the grace to lead in His kingdom is a call to serve. Despite the perverted pious view of leadership which has emerged in many nations, the example of Christ, which He modeled and imparted to His disciples, was one of servanthood. Matthew, Mark, and Luke all record a similar occasion when Jesus answered the question, "Who is the greatest?" Apparently, a dispute had arisen among the disciples as to "Who then is greatest in the kingdom of heaven?" (Matthew 18:1). We see this same mentality concerning greatness today. But this is not the way of our Lord and His Kingdom, and Jesus seizes the occasion to establish childlike humility as the essential quality for determining greatness within His Kingdom. Read Mathew 18:1-5.

Mark 9:33-37 adds more detail as Jesus further clarifies who is greatest in His kingdom. Mark 9:35 reveals, "And He sat down, called the twelve, and said to them, 'If anyone desires to be first, he shall be last of all and servant of all.'" Greatness, Jesus teaches, requires humility and deference as the mentality of a faithful servant. Luke 9:46-48 adds to this essential quality of leading well when Jesus stresses that those who are least among us are those who are most significant. Read Luke 9:48.

Like Ham, a son of Noah, Jesus came as the "servant of servants" (Genesis 9:25). In Mark 10:45, Jesus testifies, "For even the Son of Man did not come to be served, but to serve, and to give His life a ransom for many." Read Philippians 2:5-8, where Paul instructs us to have the same mentality as did Christ.

Those who would write the epistles described themselves as:

- A bondservant of Jesus Christ (Romans 1:1)
- Bondservants of Jesus Christ (Philippians 1:1)
- A bondservant of God (Titus 1:1)

- A prisoner of Christ (Philemon 1:1)
- A bondservant of God and of the Lord Jesus Christ (James 1:1)
- A bondservant (2 Peter 1)
- A bondservant of Jesus Christ (Jude 1:1)

Leading as a servant is an accurate measure of leading well. Throughout the Word of God, those who got it right were those who realized that their call to lead was a call to serve. Although their servant-leadership expressed itself through the lives of others, they were serving the Lord. Leading as a servant is essentially ministry to the Lord. You are called to Him and to His agenda. Servants of the Lord limit themselves like Jesus to the Father's will. Read John 8:26, 28, and 38.

WORD INSIGHT
Bondservant (Strong's 1401) (doulos from deo = to bind) was an individual bound to another in servitude and conveys the idea of the slave's close, binding ties with his master, belonging to him, obligated to and desiring to do his will and in a permanent relation of servitude. In sum, the will of the doulos is consumed in the will of the master. In the Greek culture, doulos usually referred to the

involuntary, permanent service of a slave. But the use in the epistles of Paul and Peter elevates the meaning of doulos to the Hebrew sense, which describes a servant who willingly commits himself to serve a master he loves and respects (cp Exodus 21:5, 6 Deuteronomy 15:12-16). Doulos speaks of submission to one's master. The doulos had no life of his own, no will of his own, no purpose of his own, and no plan of his own. All was subject to his master. The bondservant's every thought, breath, and effort was subject to the will of his master. A bondservant is one who surrendered wholly to another's will and thus devoted to another to the disregard of his own interest. In sum, the picture of a bondservant is one who is absolutely surrendered and totally devoted to his master. What an example for all believers of every age to emulate! This word provides an incredible word picture of those who are bound to their Lord Jesus Christ, Who had bought them with a price to be His own possession. (*Precept Commentary*)

All of this, along with Jesus' example and teaching in John 13:1-17, shatter the proud, arrogant, boastful, entitled, and idolatrous image of leadership that has emerged, especially in our nation. Leaders who lead well demonstrate their significance through Christ-like humility, service, and deference. Godly leadership is the antithesis of what is prized and celebrated and condoned as leadership by many people today. God's way cuts against the grain. Godly leaders have to remain humble and buffet their flesh daily. Opportunities abound to become proud or be led by evil ambition. Yet those who desire to hear our Lord say, "Well done, my good and faithful servant," must resist them all. Choose to lead as a servant. The quality of servanthood must be a primary focal point of all those desiring to lead and finish well.

Questions: What from this one devotional entry has impacted you most? How so? How has this entire process impacted you most? How would you rate your resolve to pay the price for leading well?

Application: List seven qualities that you intend to institute immediately in your leadership function. How will you do so? When will you do so? How will you measure your success? Who will hold you accountable?

Prayer: *Father, I thank You that You sent Your Son as our Example and Model for all things. He is the epitome of a* *servant in Your Kingdom. Cause me to follow His example in serving others. May the characteristics He exhibited be a consistent part of who I am. I pray that you help me demonstrate the grace of leadership You have given me to serve others. I desire to lead and finish well as our Lord Jesus did. So, I humbly ask that You enable me to pay the price of being a faithful servant and hear You speak those words over me when I stand before you, "Well done, my good and faithful servant. Enter into the joy of the Lord." Amen.*

The End - Finish Well!

"Jesus said to them, "My food is to do the will of Him who sent Me, and to finish His work." (John 4:34)

"I have glorified You on the earth. I have finished the work which You have given Me to do." (John 17:4)

"It is not always about how you start. What is most important is how you finish!" Reginald M. Holiday

"But none of these things move me; nor do I count my life dear to myself, so that I may finish my race with joy, and the ministry which I received from the Lord Jesus, to testify to the gospel of the grace of God." (Acts 20:24)

I want to reiterate this thought. Leading well is not about a destination but a journey. It is the process and culmination of a lifetime of leadership function. It is not so much about arriving as it is about becoming. Leading well is about making mistakes but learning and growing from them. It is about making tough decisions getting some of them right, getting a few of them wrong but improving from them all. It is about navigating challenges and disappointments and even betrayal. Leading well is about handling rejection and being misunderstood or unappreciated but leading anyway. It is about all of these things yet going forward despite them all. Leading well requires a lot out of us!

Leading well is about seeing Jesus Christ as the ultimate example of leadership function and seeking to imitate Him. It is about developing one's self. It is about being transformed and led by the Holy Spirit. Leading well is about valuing and developing others. It is about making people and places better than they were before you arrived. Leading well is about demonstrating compassion along with your leadership. It is about working selflessly with others and building quality teams that get more done together than they do apart. Leading well is about raising successors. It understands that success is not a success if there are no successors. It is about leading with an end in mind. Leading well is about putting all the pieces together and working them. It is about leadership function operating as near its full potential as possible yet striving still to get better and benefit many others. I hope and pray a new passion is beginning to burn in you right now!

In Acts 20:24, Paul speaks of the resolve leading well necessitates. He says, "But none of these things move me; nor do I count my life dear to myself, so that I may finish my race with joy, and the ministry which I received from the Lord Jesus, to testify to the gospel of the grace of God." He spoke explicitly of the chains and tribulation of which the Holy Spirit testified awaited him in every city (Acts 20:23). He was so compelled to lead well, to finish his race, and complete his stewardship (2 Timothy 4:6-8). He exemplifies to us one of the essential qualities for leading well – RESOLVE. Paul so believed in Christ and His kingdom that no cost was too high for him to pay. What about you? Do you believe in what you are doing and where you lead to a similar degree that you are willing to pay the price for "good success"? John Maxwell includes this as one of the *17 Indisputable Laws of Teamwork* and calls this *the Law of the Price Tag,* which says the team fails to reach its potential when it fails to pay the price. I believe this is true for us individually as leaders. Meaning, you will not realize your potential if you fail to personally pay the price tag, which begins with your willingness to do so, not knowing the price. Being willing to pay the price was the resolve that Paul had. Those who lead well must possess this too.

Look at how Paul described the things he had endured as a part of his leadership function. "For I think that God has displayed us, the apostles, last, as men condemned to death; for we have been made a spectacle to the world, both to angels and to men. We are fools for Christ's sake, but you are wise in Christ! We are weak, but you are strong! You are distinguished, but we are dishonored! To the present hour we both hunger and thirst, and we are poorly clothed, and beaten, and homeless. And we labor, working with our own hands. Being reviled, we bless; being persecuted, we endure; being defamed, we entreat. We have been made as the filth of the world, the offscouring of all things until now" (1 Corinthians 4:9-13). See also 2 Corinthians 6:4-10. Talking about resolve and commitment! There are not too many snapshots that eclipse this one by Paul. Are you willing to do whatever it takes to lead well? (That which is lawful and right only!)

Leading well also requires that we lead with an end in mind. Leading with an end in mind is what we read of Paul. Leading in this manner is also what we saw of Christ and others. They all had a view to an end. Peter admonished the saints, "But the end of all things is at hand; therefore be serious and watchful in your prayers. And above all things have fervent love for one another, for "love will cover a multitude of sins. Be hospitable to one another without grumbling. As each one has received a gift, minister it to one another, as good stewards of the manifold grace of God. If anyone speaks, let him speak as the oracles of God. If anyone ministers, let him do it as with the ability which God supplies, that in all things God may be glorified through Jesus Christ, to whom belong the glory and the dominion forever and ever. Amen" (1 Peter 4:7-11). The "end" speaks to a place of accountability, a point of evaluation where who we have been and what we have done will be scrutinized. In this manner is how we must lead. We must also instruct others in this way. There will be an accounting. See 2 Corinthians 5:9-11.

Every leader intending to lead well must apply these things to their ongoing leadership function, modeling them before others while assisting and urging them to rise to the standard of the Lord.

For the Christian, just like our elder brother, Christ, we want to do all things well (Mark 7:37). We want ultimately to hear the Lord say "well" done, My good and faithful servant (See Matthew 25:21). I believe we find what He desires and His will in His Word, which depicts what He wants us to be and do. And we must lead according to His Word if we aim to lead well. But more than anything, we want to become the person the Father has eternally ordained. I cannot stress this enough! We must enjoy the process of getting there as much as the arrival. But we cannot be in error about what the actual destination is. It is who we become in Him, which is what this is all about.

As we come to the end of our time together, I hope that the reader will be more and more inclined to lead in such a way that God will commend them for having #LeadWell!" How did I do? How do you see your leadership function now compared to when you began this process? More importantly, how do you now view yourself?

My prayer for you is what the writer of Hebrew penned to the saints,

"Now may the God of peace [Who is the Author and the Giver of peace], Who brought again from among the dead our Lord Jesus, that great Shepherd of the sheep, by the blood that [sealed, ratified] the everlasting agreement (covenant testament), Strengthen (complete, perfect) and make you what you ought to be and equip you with everything good that you may carry out His will; [while He Himself] works in you and accomplishes that which is pleasing in His sight, through Jesus Christ (the Messiah) to Whom be the glory forever and ever (to the ages of the ages). Amen (so be it). (Hebrews 13:20, 21 Amplified)

Congratulations! You made it! You are on your way to leading well each day and for a lifetime if you stick with it.

What have you learned? How were you challenged? How will you maintain the growth you have experienced? What will you do with what you have learned? With whom will you share what you now know? What will you do next? A lot of questions, huh? It is all intentional. You have made a tremendous investment in yourself. My prayer for you is that you experienced an incremental harvest of the time you have sown along the way. But do not stop here!

Finishing this Leadership Development Devotion is prayerfully a catalyst for an even more significant investment. Return to this book from time to time and dig even deeper into each topic. Please share it with another person, perhaps your spouse, your children, your team, etc.

Finally, I urge you to view "the finish" as a Person and not as an event. Your development is about you becoming the person that God has ordained. It is also a call for you to recognize and function going forward as one who will not be satisfied until they are consistently becoming more like the most excellent leader ever, the Lord Jesus Christ. We are not "finished" until we are just like Him! #LeadWell!

For those who may not know Jesus Christ as Savior and Lord

Just in case you have never asked Jesus Christ to forgive you of your sins and give you eternal life, I encourage you to repent to the Father for all the sins in your life. Then believe in the finished work of Jesus Christ. Know and believe that He has done everything for you to be forgiven and made right with the Father. Get baptized in water. And receive the Holy Spirit. If you need help with this or have any questions, please contact us, and we will be more than glad to assist you. These steps are vital to anyone who desires to finish well and has never taken them before this moment.

To those of you already a part of the Family of God, I pray that this book, as you apply its teachings, will help you accurately and adequately represent the Christ. I also pray those you lead will benefit and be blessed as they receive from your leadership function. **#LeadWell!**

Twenty Must-Read Leadership Books

1. *The Emotionally Healthy Leader*, by Peter Scazzero
2. *Who's Holding Your Ladder*, by Samuel Chand
3. 360 Leader, by John Maxwell
4. *African American Church Leadership*, by Lee June and Christopher Mathis, Jr.
5. *Leadership Pain*, by Samuel Chand
6. *Spiritual Leadership*, by Henry & Richard Blackaby
7. *The Leadership Challenge*, by Kouzes & Posner
8. *Spiritual Leadership*, by J. Oswald Chambers
9. *Survive, Thrive or Dive*, by Kevin J.A. Orieux
10. *Effective Keys to Successful Leadership*, by Frank Damazio
11. *The Spirit of Leadership*, by Myles Munroe
12. *21 Irrefutable Laws of Leadership*, by John Maxwell
13. *The Making of a Leader*, by Frank Damazio
14. *In Charge*, by Myles Munroe
15. *Empowering Leadership*, by Michael Fletcher
16. *Power to Follow, Grace to Lead*, by David L. McKenna
17. *4C Leadership: Lessons Learned from the COVID Crisis*, by Courtney McBath
18. *Character: The Path God Walks*, by Eric L. Warren
19. *YOLO: You Only Lead One*, by Jonathan M. Leath
20. *The Top Ten Mistakes Leaders Make*, Hans Finzel

About the Author

Reginald M. Holiday is a servant of the Lord. His God-given call is to build the Father's house. He has been faithfully married to his lovely wife, best friend, and ministry partner, Linda, for over thirty-two years. She is the mother of their three sons and one daughter. They have one son-in-law, two daughters-in-law, and seven grandchildren.

Together, the Holidays lead *On Target Equipping Group*, which exists to "help the saints to hit God's Target" (Eph. 4:13) and conduct leadership and ministry development and training and marriage and pre-marriage coaching.

He is a member of the Elders' Team of Bethany Fellowship Church, located in Greensboro, NC. This life-giving fellowship of Christians is a local and global, equipping, and sending center that seeks to fully embrace New Testament devotion, doctrine, order, and practice.

He is also a founding member and serves as an apostolic leader of Pneuma Ministries International Inc. (www.pneuma-ministries.com), a family of New Testament Churches and Ministry gifts that desire to see other ministry gifts equipped and New Testament churches established in the United States and abroad.

URGENT PLEA!

Thank You For Reading My Book!

I really appreciate all of your feedback, and

I love hearing what you have to say.

I need your input to make the next version of this book and

my future books better.

Please leave me a helpful review on Amazon, letting me

know what you thought of the book.

Thanks so much!!

~ Reginald Holiday ~

Made in the USA
Columbia, SC
22 September 2022

67792808R00111